UNITED NATIONS CONFERENCE ON TR

EXPROPRIATION

**UNCTAD Series on Issues in International Investment
Agreements II**

UNITED NATIONS
New York and Geneva, 2012

NOTE

As the focal point in the United Nations system for investment and technology, and building on 30 years of experience in these areas, UNCTAD, through the Division on Investment and Enterprise (DIAE), promotes understanding of key issues, particularly matters related to foreign direct investment (FDI). DIAE assists developing countries in attracting and benefiting from FDI by building their productive capacities, enhancing their international competitiveness and raising awareness about the relationship between investment and sustainable development. The emphasis is on an integrated policy approach to investment and enterprise development.

The term "country" as used in this study also refers, as appropriate, to territories or areas. The designations employed and the presentation of the material do not imply the expression of any opinion whatsoever on the part of the Secretariat of the United Nations concerning the legal status of any country, territory, city or area or of its authorities, or concerning the delimitation of its frontiers or boundaries. In addition, the designations of country groups are intended solely for statistical or analytical convenience and do not necessarily express a judgment about the stage of development reached by a particular country or area in the development process.

The following symbols have been used in the tables:

Two dots (..) indicate that data are not available or are not separately reported.

Rows in tables have been omitted in those cases where no data are available for any of the elements in the row.

A dash (–) indicates that the item is equal to zero or its value is negligible.

A blank in a table indicates that the item is not applicable.

A slash (/) between dates representing years, e.g. 1994/1995, indicates a financial year.

Use of a dash (–) between dates representing years, e.g. 1994–1995, signifies the full period involved, including the beginning and end years.

Reference to "dollars" ($) means United States dollars, unless otherwise indicated.

Annual rates of growth or change, unless otherwise stated, refer to annual compound rates.

Details and percentages in tables do not necessarily add to totals because of rounding.

The material contained in this study may be freely quoted with appropriate acknowledgement.

UNCTAD/DIAE/IA/2011/7

UNITED NATIONS PUBLICATION
Sales No. E.12.II.D.7
ISBN 978-92-1-112847-5
e-ISBN 978-92-1-055417-6

PREFACE

This volume is part of a series of revised editions – sequels – to UNCTAD's Series on Issues in International Investment Agreements. The first generation of this series (also called the Pink Series) was published between 1999 and 2005 as part of UNCTAD's work programme on international investment agreements (IIAs). It aimed at helping developing countries to participate as effectively as possible in international investment rulemaking at the bilateral, regional, plurilateral and multilateral levels. The series sought to provide balanced analyses of issues that may arise in discussions about IIAs, and has since then become a standard reference tool for IIA negotiators, policymakers, the private sector, academia and other stakeholders.

Since the publication of the first generation of the Pink Series, the world of IIAs has changed tremendously. In terms of numbers, the IIAs' universe has grown, and continues to do so – albeit to a lesser degree. Also, the impact of IIAs has evolved. Many investor-State dispute settlement (ISDS) cases have brought to light unanticipated – and partially undesired – side effects of IIAs. With its expansive – and sometimes contradictory – interpretations, the arbitral interpretation process has created a new learning environment for countries and, in particular, for IIA negotiators. Issues of transparency, predictability and policy space have come to the forefront of the debate. So has the objective of ensuring coherence between IIAs and other areas of public policy, including policies to address global challenges such as the protection of the environment (climate change) or public health and safety. Finally, the underlying dynamics of IIA rulemaking have changed. A rise in South-South FDI flows and the emerging economies' growing role as outward investors – also with respect to the developed world – are beginning to alter the context and background against which IIAs are being negotiated.

It is the purpose of the sequels to consider how the issues described in the first-generation Pink Series have evolved, particularly focusing on treaty practice and the process of arbitral interpretation. Each of the sequels will have similar key elements, including (a) an introduction explaining the issue in today's broader context, (b) a stocktaking of IIA practice and arbitral awards and (c) a section on policy options for IIA negotiators, offering language for possible new clauses that better take into account the development needs of host countries and enhance the stability and predictability of the legal system.

The updates are conceptualized as sequels, i.e. they aim to complement rather than replace the first-generation Pink Series. Compared with the first-generation, the sequels will offer a greater level of detail and move beyond a merely informative role. In line with UNCTAD's mandate, they will aim at analysing the development impact and strengthening the development dimension of IIAs. The sequels are complementary to UNCTAD's Investment Policy Framework for Sustainable Development (IPFSD), providing an in-depth analysis of particular topics covered in the IPFSD. The sequels are finalized through a rigorous process of peer reviews, which benefits from collective learning and the sharing of experiences. Attention is placed on ensuring the involvement of a broad set of stakeholders, aiming to capture ideas and concerns from society at large.

This sequel was edited by Anna Joubin-Bret, and produced by a team under the direction of Jörg Weber and the overall guidance of James Zhan. The members of the team include Wolfgang Alschner, Bekele Amare, Dolores Bentolila, Anna Lisa Brahms, Hamed El-Kady, Natalia Guerra, Jan Knoerich, Sergey Ripinsky, Diana Rosert, Claudia Salgado, Ileana Tejada and Elisabeth Tuerk.

This paper is based on a study prepared by Alejandro Faya, Anna Joubin-Bret and Sergey Ripinsky. Claudia Salgado provided inputs. The UNCTAD secretariat gratefully acknowledges the comments on the draft version of this paper received from Andrea Bjorklund, Geraldine Fischer, Norah Gallagher, Gus van Harten, Peter Muchlinski, Stephan Schill and Brigitte Stern. The paper should not be seen as representing the views of any of the afore-mentioned peer reviewers. The research was facilitated by access to the Investor-State Law Guide (ISLG) database.

The paper was typeset and formatted by Teresita Ventura. Sophie Combette designed the cover.

Supachai Panitchpakdi
Secretary-General of UNCTAD

July 2012

CONTENTS

BOXES

ABBREVIATIONS

ASEAN	Association of Southeast Asian Nations
BIT	bilateral investment treaty
CAFTA-DR	Dominican Republic-Central America-United States Free Trade Agreement
CEPA	comprehensive economic partnership agreement
COMESA	Common Market for Eastern and Southern Africa
DCF	discounted cash flow
EPA	economic partnership agreement
EU	European Union
FDI	foreign direct investment
FET	fair and equitable treatment
FTA	free trade agreement
GATS	General Agreement on Trade in Services
GATT	General Agreement on Tariffs and Trade
ICC	International Chamber of Commerce
ICJ	International Court of Justice
ICSID	International Centre for Settlement of Investment Disputes
IIA	international investment agreement
IPR	intellectual property right
ISDS	investor-State dispute settlement
LIBOR	London Interbank Offered Rate
MAI	Multilateral Agreement on Investment
NAFTA	North American Free Trade Agreement
OECD	Organisation for Economic Cooperation and Development
TNC	transnational corporation
VAT	value added tax
WTO	World Trade Organization

EXECUTIVE SUMMARY

The protection of foreign investors from uncompensated expropriations traditionally has been one of the main guarantees found in international investment agreements (IIAs). Direct takings involve the transfer of title and/or outright physical seizure of the property. Some measures short of physical takings may also amount to takings in that they permanently destroy the economic value of the investment or deprive the owner of its ability to manage, use or control its property in a meaningful way. These measures are categorized as indirect expropriations. Finally, there are also non-discriminatory regulatory measures, i.e. acts taken by States in the exercise of their right to regulate in the public interest that may lead to effects similar to indirect expropriation but at the same time are not classified as expropriation and do not give rise to the obligation to compensate those affected.

Investors may bring expropriation claims with respect to any conduct that is attributable to the host State and in which the latter engaged in its sovereign capacity. As regards the types of assets that can be expropriated, IIAs typically refer to investments; this enhances the importance of a suitable definition of the term "investment" in the agreements. Some recent IIAs have specifically narrowed down the range of assets capable of being expropriated to tangible and intangible property rights and property interests in investment.

Where a measure affects a discrete economic right or an individual asset, the outcome of the expropriation analysis may depend on whether the asset concerned will be viewed as an investment or whether the investor's overall business or enterprise is viewed as such. In making this assessment, an important factor is whether the right concerned is capable of economic exploitation independently of the remainder of the business. The nature and validity of rights or interests that are alleged to have been expropriated must be assessed in light of the laws and regulations of the recipient country of investment.

An overwhelming majority of IIAs allow States to expropriate investments as long as the taking is effected for a public purpose, in a non-discriminatory manner, under due process of law and against the payment of compensation. In the past years, a number of arbitral decisions have discussed these conditions helping to further flesh out their meaning. One of the more difficult questions has been whether the non-payment of compensation alone can render the expropriation unlawful. It appears that while a failure by a State to pay any compensation for a direct expropriation can be seen as unlawful, this should not be the case of an indirect expropriation. Given that the expropriatory nature of the measure is established at the time of the tribunal's decision, the obligation to pay compensation should be deemed to arise only from the time of such finding.

In recent years, the evolution of the economic and regulatory environment has brought to the forefront questions regarding indirect expropriations. They concern the appropriate criteria that allow (a) to determine whether an indirect taking has occurred and (b) to distinguish indirect expropriation from regulation in the public interest, which is non-compensable despite the economic impact on particular investments. Many of these questions have been addressed by States in recent IIAs that clarify relevant criteria.

These new clarificatory provisions typically provide for a case-by-case balancing of factors, which include the economic impact of the measure, interference with distinct and reasonable investment-backed expectations and nature and characteristics of the measure. The economic impact must be equivalent to that of a direct expropriation, i.e. amount to a total or near-total deprivation. With respect to investors' expectations, those would typically be considered distinct and reasonable where they are based on written commitments of the State concerned.

The nature and characteristics of a particular measure has emerged as a key factor in drawing a line between indirect expropriation and non-compensable regulation. A bona fide regulatory act (or its application to an individual investor) that genuinely pursues a legitimate public-policy objective (such as the protection of the environment and public health and safety) and complies with the requirements of non-discrimination, due process and proportionality may not be designated as expropriatory, despite an adverse economic impact. This follows from the doctrine of police powers of States which, in its contemporary meaning, goes well beyond the fundamental functions of custody, security and protection and encompasses the full regulatory dimension of States. It effectively places the risks arising from bona fide regulation on economic actors.

While the general conceptual framework regarding indirect takings is grounded in customary international law and has been clarified in recent treaties and arbitral awards, some of its individual elements are subject to debate. In particular, the role of the proportionality approach and the criterion of direct economic benefit to the State may require further elaboration and discussion.

Another key topic concerns compensation. While in theory, compensation for lawful expropriation should be different from reparation for an unlawful one, in many cases the two are determined by reference to the same fair market value of the expropriated investment. From the policy perspective, it may be useful to allow factoring in specific circumstances of the case and equitable considerations when determining compensation for lawful expropriation. Under this approach, the fair market value of the investment would serve as a starting point only. These considerations are particularly relevant in cases of indirect expropriations that do not necessarily entail a transfer of economic benefit from an investor to a State. As the practice of European Court of Human Rights shows, the concept of proportionality may also have a role to play in this determination.

Negotiators of IIAs have at their disposal a range of policy options. This paper's discussion of various issues may help in developing expropriation provisions that would take into account the existing experience, respond to specific policy concerns, provide a required degree of predictability and eventually be conducive to sustainable economic development.

INTRODUCTION

States have a sovereign right under international law to take property held by nationals or aliens through nationalization or expropriation for economic, political, social or other reasons. In order to be lawful, the exercise of this sovereign right requires, under international law, that the following conditions be met:

(a) Property has to be taken for a public purpose;
(b) On a non-discriminatory basis;
(c) In accordance with due process of law;
(d) Accompanied by compensation.

While the right of States to expropriate is recognized as a fundamental one, the exercise by States of this right has triggered conflicts, debates and disagreements that are far from over, although the tone and content, coupled with the procedural means to settle disputes, have varied significantly over time.

In the first part of the twentieth century, the first major phase of mass expropriations (nationalizations) occurred during revolutionary movements in Russia and Mexico. A second wave of nationalizations and expropriations followed the period of decolonization that took place after the Second World War. The debate was then focused on the States' right to economic self-determination, including the right to expropriate without "full compensation", but rather by granting "appropriate compensation" (UNCTAD, 2000, pp. 5–7; Dugan et al., 2008, p. 435).

Since then, few measures of outright expropriation have been taken by States and challenged by investors. In recent times, the concept of indirect expropriation, although not a new category of takings, found unprecedented fertile ground. This trend is explained by two factors: (a) investors' rights are now enshrined in numerous IIAs concluded in the past 50 years, which make it possible for them to directly challenge the conduct of host States, and (b) States tend to intervene more frequently in the economy, and some of their actions may have a negative impact on the economic interests of private actors.

The evolution of the economic and regulatory environment has become particularly visible with the recent global financial crisis. It highlighted the role of States in devising policies and taking measures in the public interest. States have intervened to rescue entire sectors of the economy and have taken stakes in companies, including transnational corporations (TNCs). (UNCTAD, 2010, pp. 79–81). States are also expected to take responsible measures to regulate issues of public health, social welfare and safety, as well as to protect the environment and public welfare.

The first edition of the IIA paper, *Taking of Property* (UNCTAD, 2000), looked into direct and indirect expropriation. It identified and analysed expropriations that do not trigger the international responsibility of the State as long as certain requirements are met. It also looked into the State's legitimate right to regulate in the public interest, which may at times result in the loss of the economic value of investments, without amounting to an expropriation, and therefore, without requiring compensation.

In recent years, the notions of indirect expropriation and regulatory takings, the way they are established, their content and the applicable standards of compensation have evolved and have been further clarified. IIAs have also become more precise and detailed in:

(a) Defining the types of measures that can or cannot constitute indirect expropriation;
(b) Devising exceptions to protect the space for States to regulate in the public interest;

(c) Indicating valuation methods for measuring compensation.

This sequel examines recent treaty practice regarding expropriation as well as recent arbitral awards applying and interpreting these treaty provisions. It aims to offer solutions to the existing interpretative issues as well as to provide policy options for future treaties.

The paper proceeds as follows. Section I defines the concepts of direct and indirect expropriation and reviews the variety of measures that can constitute an expropriation. It discusses what economic rights and interests may constitute an object of a taking. This section also reviews in detail the conditions for an expropriation to be lawful, namely public purpose, non-discrimination, due process and payment of compensation.

Section II focuses on the core issue of establishing an indirect expropriation: the recent treaty practice with regard to defining indirect expropriation as well as arbitral practice with regard to assessing the impact of a measure, its interference with an investor's reasonable investment-backed expectations and the nature, character and objectives of the measure. The section goes on to examine criteria that can facilitate the differentiation between indirect expropriation and normal exercise of police and regulatory powers by States. It concludes by presenting a framework for analysis (a sequence of analytical steps) that can be applied to determine whether a measure constitutes an indirect expropriation

Section III discusses the differences between compensation for a lawful expropriation and reparation for unlawful expropriations, as well as the question of valuation of investments.

Section IV offers options that policymakers and negotiators may wish to consider. Proposed policy options include the granting of full and unfettered protection to foreign investors as well clarifications of criteria, approaches and methodology to assess an allegedly expropriatory measure. It pays particular attention to specific exceptions and limitations that can be included. Section IV is followed by conclusions based on the study.

I. CATEGORIES OF EXPROPRIATION, REQUISITE ELEMENTS AND CONDITIONS OF LAWFULNESS

Through IIAs, States have established a guarantee for foreign investors against the expropriation of their investments without compensation. Today virtually all bilateral investment treaties (BITs) contain an expropriation provision. Customary international law also contains rules on the expropriation of foreign-owned property and continues to supplement IIAs on those issues where the latter leave gaps or require interpretation.

The IIA terminology on takings is not fully consistent. Different terms, such as expropriation, taking, nationalization, deprivation and dispossession, can be encountered. These terms are often used interchangeably; their use typically depends on legal tradition and translation.

Nationalization usually refers to massive or large-scale takings of private property in all economic sectors or on an industry – or sector-specific basis. Outright nationalizations in all economic sectors are generally motivated by policy considerations; the measures are intended to achieve complete State control of the economy and involve the takeover of all privately owned means of production. Many former colonies regarded nationalizations as an integral part of their decolonization process in the period following the end of the Second World War. Nationalizations on an industry-wide basis take place when a government seeks to reorganize a particular industry by taking over the private enterprises in the industry and creating a State monopoly. In these cases, the assets taken become publicly owned.

Expropriations generally refer to property-specific or enterprise-specific takings where the property rights remain with the

State or are transferred by the State to other economic operators.
Expropriations may consist of a large-scale taking of land by the
State, made with the purpose of redistributing it, or specific takings
where the target is a specific foreign firm (for example, a firm
dominating a market or industry) or a specific plot of land (for
example, to build a highway).

Both nationalizations and expropriations, if they are direct,
involve the transfer of title and/or outright physical seizure of the
property. However, some measures short of physical takings may
also amount to takings in that they permanently destroy the
economic value of the investment or deprive the owner of its ability
to manage, use or control its property in a meaningful way. These
measures are categorized as indirect expropriations. Finally, there
are also regulatory measures, i.e. acts taken by States in the exercise
of their right to regulate in public interest. These measures will
typically not give rise to compensation, even though they may have
the same effects as an indirect expropriation.

The following three sections discuss these categories of
measures in some more detail. The chapter then looks at the types of
State acts that have been challenged before an IIA tribunal and
explores the question of rights that are capable of being
expropriated. Finally, this chapter will examine the conditions for an
expropriation to be lawful which are found in both customary
international law and IIAs.

A. Direct expropriation

Direct expropriation means a mandatory legal transfer of the
title to the property or its outright physical seizure. Normally, the
expropriation benefits the State itself or a State-mandated third
party.

In cases of direct expropriation, there is an open, deliberate and unequivocal intent, as reflected in a formal law or decree or physical act, to deprive the owner of his or her property through the transfer of title or outright seizure.

Today large-scale direct expropriations (nationalizations) are rare, although some countries in Latin America have recently resorted to such measures. States have also taken emergency measures, involving acquisitions of large parts of capital, to rescue some sectors of the economy affected by the global financial and economic crisis of 2008–2009.

B. Indirect expropriation

Indirect expropriation involves total or near-total deprivation of an investment but without a formal transfer of title or outright seizure. The notion was recognized in international law long before the appearance of investment treaties. Half a century ago one scholar noted that "*there are several well-known international cases in which it has been recognized that property rights may be so interfered with that it may be said that to all intents and purposes those property rights have been expropriated even though the State in question has not purported to expropriate*" (Christie, 1962, p. 310).

In some early judicial and arbitral decisions, such as the *Case concerning certain German Interests in Polish Upper Silesia* (the *Chorzów Factory* case) [1] and the *Norwegian Shipowners' Claims* case,[2] it was found that a State measure can constitute an indirect expropriation. Likewise, the Iran-United States Claims Tribunal repeatedly referred to the existence of indirect expropriation under international law and identified a number of tests in that respect. A classical definition can be found in the *Starrett Housing* case:

"...*it is recognized under international law that **measures taken by a State can interfere with property rights to such an extent that these rights are rendered so useless that they must be deemed to have been expropriated**, even though the State does not purport to have expropriated them and the legal title to the property formally remains with the original owner.*"[3] (Emphasis added.)

In recent years, the vast majority of IIAs have referred to both direct and indirect expropriation. Only few treaties of the later generation do not refer explicitly to indirect expropriation or measures having equivalent effect. This is for example the case of the Lebanon-Malaysia (BIT) (2003),[4] which provides the following:

"*Neither Contracting Party shall take any measures of expropriation or nationalization against the investments of an investor of the other Contracting Party except under the following conditions...*"

Similarly, the Austria-Croatia BIT (1997) states:

"*Investments of investors of either Contracting Party shall not be expropriated in the territory of the other Contracting Party except for a public purpose by due process of law and against compensation...*".

It can be argued that even when an IIA does not specifically mention indirect takings, the notion of expropriation is broad enough to cover relevant measures of both direct and indirect kind.

Most IIAs, however, explicitly refer to both direct and indirect expropriations in one way or another. The most common way of doing this is by using phrases such as "equivalent to" or "tantamount to". The examples in box 1 illustrate the references to indirect expropriation in recent IIAs.

In some IIAs, negotiators have sought to give a more detailed definition of direct and indirect expropriations. For example, the Dominican Republic-Central America Free Trade Agreement (CAFTA-DR) (2006) in annex 10-C draws a distinction between direct and indirect expropriation:

> "*3. Article 10.7.1 addresses two situations. The first is direct expropriation, where an investment is nationalized or otherwise directly expropriated through formal transfer of title or outright seizure.*
>
> *4. The second situation addressed by article 10.7.1 is indirect expropriation, where an action or series of actions by a Party has an effect equivalent to direct expropriation without formal transfer of title or outright seizure.*"

The approach taken in this and other similar treaties (Australia-Chile Free Trade Agreement (FTA) (2006), Japan-Philippines FTA (2008) and others) is to clearly define what constitutes a direct and indirect expropriation and set out criteria for finding an indirect taking. Section II of this sequel will further examine the factors that allow determining whether a measure or series of measures constitute an indirect expropriation.

Issues relating to indirect expropriation have been addressed by the European Court of Human Rights. It has been discussed in other instruments, including the Harvard Draft Convention on the International Responsibility of States for Injury to Aliens (1961) and the Third Restatement of Foreign Relations Law of the United States (1987). Although these two documents are not binding, they are considered to be an influential element of doctrine (Organisation for Economic Cooperation and Development (OECD), 2004, p. 6).

Box 1. Reference to indirect expropriation

Egypt-Germany BIT (2005)

Article 4. Expropriation

"[...]

2) Investments by investors of either Contracting State shall not directly or indirectly be expropriated, nationalized or subjected to any other measures the effects of which would be tantamount to expropriation or nationalization in the territory of the other Contracting State except for the public benefit and against compensation...." (Emphasis added.)

Mexico-United Kingdom BIT (2006)

Article 7. Expropriation

"*Investments of investors of either Contracting Party shall not be nationalized or expropriated, either directly or indirectly through measures having effect equivalent to nationalization or expropriation ("expropriation") in the territory of the other Contracting Party except for a public purpose, on a non-discriminatory basis, in accordance with due process of law and against compensation....*" (Emphasis added.)

Japan-Lao People's Democratic Republic BIT (2008)

Article 12. Expropriation and Compensation

"*1. Neither Contracting Party shall expropriate or nationalize investments in its Area of investors of the other Contracting Party or take any* **measure equivalent** *to expropriation or nationalisation (hereinafter referred to as "expropriation") except: (a) for a public purpose; (b) in a non-discriminatory manner; (c) upon payment of prompt, adequate and effective compensation pursuant to paragraphs 2, 3 and 4; and (d) in accordance with due process of law and Article 5....*" (Emphasis added.)

The terminology is not fully uniform and one can encounter references to de facto, creeping, constructive, disguised, consequential, regulatory or virtual expropriation (Weston, 1976, pp. 105–106; Stern 2008, pp. 38–39). All of these are equivalents or subcategories of indirect expropriation. The subcategory worth highlighting is the so-called creeping expropriation that results in a deprivation of property or a loss of control but which occurs gradually or in stages. The arbitral tribunal in *Generation Ukraine v. Ukraine* qualified this special form of expropriation as coming *"with a distinctive temporal quality in the sense that it encapsulates the situation whereby a series of acts attributable to the State over a period of time culminate in the expropriatory taking of such property"*.[5]

Creeping expropriation may be defined as the incremental encroachment on one or more of the ownership rights of a foreign investor that eventually destroys (or nearly destroys) the value of his or her investment or deprives him or her of control over the investment. A series of separate State acts, usually taken within a limited time span, are then regarded as constituent parts of the unified treatment of the investor or investment.

Recent arbitral decisions in IIA cases explored the concept of indirect expropriation, in particular with respect to regulatory measures taken by States. In *Suez v. Argentina*, the tribunal analysed whether the measures adopted by Argentina during the economic crisis of 2000–2002 constituted an indirect expropriation. It described the latter as follows:

> *"In case of an indirect expropriation, sometimes referred to as a 'regulatory taking,' host States invoke their legislative and regulatory powers to enact measures that reduce the benefits investors derive from their investments but without actually changing or cancelling investors' legal title to their assets or diminishing their control over them."*[6]

On the basis of State practice, doctrine and arbitral awards, indirect expropriations are characterized by the following cumulative elements:

(a) An act attributable to the State;
(b) Interference with property rights or other protected legal interests;
(c) Of such degree that the relevant rights or interests lose all or most of their value or the owner is deprived of control over the investment;
(d) Even though the owner retains the legal title or remains in physical possession.

Section II analyses these elements in more detail and identifies the relevant factors and tests that are used to assess whether an indirect expropriation has occurred.

While in the case of direct expropriations, the dispossession to the detriment of a private person coincides with the appropriation by a public person, indirect expropriations do not necessarily result in an increase in the State's wealth (Nouvel, 2002, p. 89).

Unlike the case of direct expropriation, typically, the State will refuse to acknowledge the expropriatory nature of the measure and will not offer compensation to the aggrieved investor. In case of a dispute, it will be the tribunal's task to identify whether the conduct at hand constitutes an expropriation. It is therefore highly advisable that parties to an IIA provide guidance to future tribunals in identifying the measures that can be deemed expropriatory.

C. Regulatory measures not amounting to expropriations

In some instances, an act or measure of the State taken in the exercise of the State's police powers or its right to regulate in the public interest can lead to a significant impairment of businesses.

The question then arises how to distinguish between an expropriatory measure and a normal (and thus non-compensable) regulatory act of State. Recent treaties have included specific clarifications in this regard.

For instance, the Colombia-India BIT (2009) states:

"Non-discriminatory regulatory actions by a Contracting Party that are designed and applied to protect legitimate public welfare objectives including the protection of health, safety and environment do not constitute expropriation or nationalization; except in rare circumstances, where those actions are so severe that they cannot be reasonably viewed as having been adopted and applied in good faith for achieving their objectives."[7]

Similar wording is found in the Canadian BITs concluded with Jordan (2009),[8] Peru (2006)[9] and the Slovak Republic (2010);[10] in the FTAs concluded between the United States and Australia (2004),[11] the Central America-Dominican Republic (2004),[12] Chile (2003)[13] and Morocco (2004);[14] in the China-Peru FTA (2009);[15] in the Investment Agreement for the Common Market for Eastern and Southern Africa (COMESA) Common Investment Area (2007)[16] and in the Turkey model BIT (2009).[17]

Arbitral tribunals have also recognized this category of measures as not giving rise to compensation. Thus, in *Saluka Investments v. Czech Republic*, the tribunal stated that *"[i]t is now established in international law that States are not liable to pay compensation to a foreign investor when, in the normal exercise of their regulatory powers, they adopt in a non-discriminatory manner bona fide regulations that are aimed at the general welfare."*[18]

Also, in *Methanex v. USA*, the tribunal acknowledged that:

"As a matter of general international law, a non-discriminatory regulation for a public purpose, which is enacted in accordance with due process and, which affects, inter alios [sic], a foreign investor or investment is not deemed expropriatory and compensable unless specific commitments had been given by the regulating government to the then putative foreign investor contemplating investment that the government would refrain from such regulation."[19]

Criteria that guide tribunals in distinguishing between non-compensable regulation and indirect expropriation are further discussed in section II.B.

D. Which measures can be challenged?

A tribunal faced with an expropriation claim needs to verify that the acts concerned are attributable to the respondent State. In many cases this will not be difficult, given that takings are typically achieved through legislative acts or administrative decrees, revocations of licences and authorizations by State organs. The conduct of a State is considered an act of that State under international law *"whether the organ exercises legislative, executive, judicial or any other functions, whatever position it holds in the organization of the State, and whatever its characterization as an organ of the central Government or of a territorial unit of the State,"*[20]

Questions of attribution may arise in connection with the expropriation of contractual rights: when a foreign investor has a contract with a State-owned entity, it may require a determination of whether the acts of such an entity can be attributed to the State. General international rules on attribution apply in this respect.

Codified in Articles 4-11 of the International Law Commission Articles on State Responsibility, they have been interpreted on several occasions by arbitral tribunals in ISDS cases[21] and analysed by commentators (Dolzer and Schreuer, 2008, pp. 195–205; Schicho, 2011; Cohen Smutny, 2005).

The range of measures that have given rise to expropriation claims is remarkably broad, encompassing:

> "...formal sector-wide transfers of ownership (nationalizations), outright seizures, the intervention of government-appointed managers, concessions and permit breaches and annulments, prejudice suffered in domestic courts, and varied forms of regulation ranging from decrees protecting endangered cacti and antiquities to bans on gasoline additives." (Coe and Rubins, 2005, pp. 607–608).

Most expropriations are a consequence of executive and administrative acts such as resolutions, decrees, revocation, cancellation or denial of concessions, permits, licences or authorizations that are necessary for the operation of a business. Expropriation can also result from legislative measures and (more rarely) judicial acts.

Measures challenged by investors as expropriatory have included confiscatory tax measures, measures prohibiting the distribution of dividends to shareholders, labour regulations prohibiting the dismissal of staff, judicial decisions, financial regulations and rules on compulsory licences. For instance, the Iran-United States Claims Tribunal found an expropriation in a number of cases that involved the appointment by the Iranian Government of temporary managers in the subsidiaries of United States companies or the acts of such appointees.[22]

In *Occidental v. Ecuador*, the tribunal noted that "*taxes can result in expropriation as can other types of regulatory measures*".[23]

(Although in that particular case no deprivation was found.) Other types of interference leading to the finding of expropriation related to the arrest or deportation of key officers/managers (*Biloune v. Ghana*) or the forced modification of corporate-contractual arrangements (*CME v. Czech Republic*).

An IIA may include special exceptions regarding certain types of measures. Many recent treaties do so with respect to compulsory licences for intellectual property rights (IPRs) in accordance with rules established by the World Trade Organization (WTO) (i.e. when a government allows the production of patented pharmaceuticals without the consent of the patent owner). For instance, the Canadian model BIT (2004) provides that:

> "*The provisions of this Article [Expropriation] shall not apply to the issuance of compulsory licenses granted in relation to intellectual property rights, or to the revocation, limitation or creation of intellectual property rights, to the extent that such issuance, revocation, limitation or creation is consistent with the WTO Agreement.*" (Article 13.5)

The exception ensures that compulsory licences will not be challenged by IPR holders as expropriating their IPRs. This norm ensures coherence between international investment law and WTO law.

Another relevant qualification encountered in some treaties refers to the procedure that must be followed when a taxation measure is being challenged. For example, the United States model BIT (2004) provides in Article 21(2):

> "*Article 6 [Expropriation] shall apply to all taxation measures, except that a claimant that asserts that a taxation measure involves an expropriation may submit a claim to arbitration under Section B only if:*

> *(a)   The claimant has first referred to the competent tax authorities of both Parties in writing the issue of whether that taxation measure involves an expropriation; and*
>
> *(b)   within 180 days after the date of such referral, the competent tax authorities of both Parties fail to agree that the taxation measure is not an expropriation."*

According to this article, if the taxation authorities come to an agreement that the measure is not expropriatory, the claimant may not proceed with its expropriation claim.

E.   What rights can be expropriated?

Correctly identifying the object of a taking is an important part of the analysis required to find an expropriation. Several questions may arise in this context:

(a) Do the relevant rights, interests or assets fall under the IIA's definition of investment?
(b) Can those rights, interests or assets be considered individually, or do they form an integral part of the overall investment, an indivisible whole?
(c) Does the investor have valid rights under the domestic law of the host State?
(d) What special requirements exist with respect to the expropriation of contractual rights?

The present section will examine these questions.

1.   Definition of investment and types of rights protected

Expropriation provisions in IIAs refer to the expropriation of "investments". The scope of assets whose expropriation can be

challenged under an investment treaty depends on how broad or
narrow the definition of an investment is in that treaty.

The words "every kind of asset" have been commonly used
by IIAs as a formula to introduce an illustrative (non-exhaustive) list
of covered investments (UNCTAD, 2011, p. 24). A vast majority of
IIAs follow this approach. Some notable exceptions, such as the
treaties concluded by Canada after 2004, contain a closed list of
assets and explicitly exclude certain kinds of assets from the
definition.

Arbitral tribunals applying IIAs, which contain the open-
ended list of covered assets, have generally favoured an expansive
concept of an investment. The decision of the arbitral tribunal in
EnCana v. Ecuador[24] provides an illustration. In that case, the
claimant challenged as expropriatory the refusal of Ecuadorian tax
authorities to pay value added tax (VAT) refunds, to which the
claimant's companies were allegedly entitled under Ecuadorian law
(there was no question of expropriation of the claimant's enterprises
themselves – they continued to operate profitably in Ecuador). The
tribunal had to decide whether a right to VAT refunds constituted an
"investment" under the Canada-Ecuador BIT. In deciding this
question, the tribunal observed that it was "*hard to imagine a
broader definition [of 'investment'] [than the one found in the
BIT]*". It pointed out that the definition explicitly covered any
"claims to money" and "returns" (also broadly defined). On this
basis the tribunal held that the right to VAT refunds in respect of
past transactions was an investment capable of being expropriated.[25]
Such a reading would not have been possible had the BIT contained
a more restrictive definition of investment or had it referred to
expropriation of "property" or "property rights".

In *Amoco v. Iran*, the Iran-United States Claims Tribunal
stated that "*expropriation … may extend to any right which can be
the object of a commercial transaction, i.e. freely sold and bought,*

and thus has a monetary value".[26] In *Pope & Talbot v. Canada*, the tribunal considered that the *"investment's access to the United States market is a property interest subject to protection under Article 1110"*,[27] given that the ability to sell softwood from British Columbia to the United States was an important element of the business. (However, it did not consider it to be a separate investment, but assessed the impact of the loss of the export business on the investor's enterprise as a whole.)

The *Methanex v. USA* tribunal held that some of these interests are relevant only for purposes of valuation, but do not constitute discrete assets that could be expropriated separately. With respect to Methanex's claims that it had lost customer base, goodwill and market share, the tribunal held that:

> *"In the view of the Tribunal, items such as goodwill and market share may ... constitute ... an element of the value of an enterprise and as such may have been covered by some of the compensation payments. Hence in a comprehensive taking, these items may figure in valuation. But it is difficult to see how they might stand alone, in a case like the one before the Tribunal."*[28] (Emphasis added.)

Similarly, in *Chemtura v. Canada* the tribunal decided that goodwill, customers and market share should be seen as part of the "overall investment" (in this case, the investor's enterprise).[29]

Some recent treaties include a clarification that *"an action or a series of actions by a Party cannot constitute an expropriation unless it interferes with a tangible or intangible property right or property interest in an investment"*. This clause was first introduced in the 2004 United States model BIT (annex B, Expropriation) and since that time has been used in various IIAs concluded by the United States. It has also been replicated in some recent IIAs concluded by other countries (e.g. see Australia-Chile FTA (2008) (annex 10-B), Malaysia-New Zealand FTA (2009) (annex 7) or the

Association of Southeast Asian Nations (ASEAN) Comprehensive
Investment Agreement (2009) (annex 2)).

This formulation narrows down the scope of economic rights
and interests that can be expropriated, compared with the term
"investment". In particular, this formulation would seem to
definitely exclude interests such as goodwill, customer base or
market share. It may also exclude licences, permits and other
government authorizations, where they do not create property rights,
as well as non-property rights such as the right of establishment
under those IIAs which grant pre-establishment rights to investors.

The term "property interest in investment" is not precisely
defined and can be subject to interpretation of varying breadth: it
could be read as referring to essential rights inherent in the property
such as the right to use or the right to dispose and/or to appurtenant
and incidental property rights such as easement. The determination
whether a particular right qualifies as a "property right" or "property
interest in investment" would have to be made in light of the
domestic law of the host State concerned.

Arbitral awards have generally endorsed the idea that
intangible rights, in particular contractual rights, can be
expropriated. In *Phillips Petroleum Co. Iran v. Iran,* the Iran-United
States Claims Tribunal concluded that an obligation to compensate
arises *"whether the property is tangible, such as real estate, or
intangible, such as contract rights".*[30] In *Starrett Housing v. Iran*,
the Tribunal held that the property interests taken comprised
physical property as well as the right to manage and complete the
project. [31] This interpretation has been echoed in many IIA
arbitrations. [32] Intangible rights also include intellectual property
rights (IPRs). There is, however, no unified view on including
intangible rights under property rights.

Investment claims can be submitted by foreign shareholders
in a domestic company. In this case, it is their shareholding, and not

the assets of the domestic company, that constitutes an investment. *GAMI Investments v. Mexico*, a claim brought under the North American Free Trade Agreement (NAFTA), provides an illustrative example. GAMI held a 14.18 per cent interest in a Mexican-incorporated company, GAM. Some of GAM's assets, namely five sugar mills, had been expropriated by governmental decree. In the award, the tribunal made it clear that GAMI's expropriation claim could only be related to "*its investment in GAM*", namely shares in the Mexican-incorporated company.[33] In the tribunal's view, this was quite different from the loss of the underlying assets – the sugar mills – suffered by GAM. It noted that in relation to GAM, the expropriation of even one sugar mill would constitute an expropriation;[34] by contrast, GAMI would have to show that the loss of that mill had an impact on its shares that was tantamount to expropriation. The claim was dismissed.

Some IIAs include a special provision that addresses the issue of taking of assets from a domestic company in which a foreign investor holds shares. For instance, the Ethiopia-Spain BIT (2006) provides in Article 5(5):

> "*Where a Contracting Party expropriates the assets of a company which is incorporated or constituted under the law in force in any part of its own territory, and in which investors of the other Contracting Party own shares, it shall ensure that the provisions of this Article are applied so as to guarantee prompt, adequate and effective compensation in respect of their investments to such investors of the other Contracting Party who are owners of those shares.*"

This type of clause may result in compensation being paid to foreign shareholders, even if only some assets are expropriated from the domestic company which does not result in the loss of full value of the shareholding. The clause thus changes the default legal position whereby a shareholder shall be compensated where his shareholding has been expropriated.

The existence, nature and validity of rights or interests that are alleged to have been expropriated must be assessed in light of the laws and regulations of the host country of the investment. As the *Suez v. Argentina* tribunal stated, *"to assess the nature of these rights in a case of alleged expropriation of contractual rights, one must look to the domestic law under which the rights were created"*.[35]

Similarly, the tribunal in *EnCana v. Ecuador* held:

"Unlike many BITs there is no express reference to the law of the host State. However for there to have been an expropriation of an investment or return (in a situation involving legal rights or claims as distinct from the seizure of physical assets) **the rights affected must exist under the law which creates them**, *in this case, the law of Ecuador."*[36] (Emphasis added.)

Whether or not specified in the treaty, it is implicit that any investment susceptible to being expropriated must be a right or asset duly constituted, defined, formed and recognized under the laws of the host State that is granting the protection under the IIA (McLachlan et al., 2007, pp. 181–183). This is due to the fact that international law of expropriation is only concerned with the protection of property rights or other economic interests and does not regulate their process of creation.

2.   Discrete or interrelated interests: partial expropriation?

A difficult question is whether a specific part of an investment may be expropriated. Many investments are constituted by a complex combination of assets, rights and interests connected by unity of economic purpose and functionality (an "indivisible whole"). As put by the *Enron v. Argentina* tribunal, *"an investment is indeed a complex process including various arrangements, such as contracts, licences and other agreements leading to the materialization of such investment..."*.[37]

Given that any expropriation analysis is required to assess the impact of a State measure on an investor's investment (see section II.A.1), it is important to determine what the investment at stake is. In particular, this may require a decision on whether a discrete affected economic right or interest, which forms part of a larger business package or overall economic activity, can be treated as an investment. A building, a piece of land or a line of business are individual assets, which may at the same time be part of the larger business structure. Where a measure negatively affects only an individual asset, the outcome of the expropriation analysis will largely depend on whether the asset concerned will be viewed as an "investment" or where the overall business or enterprise is viewed as such. While in the first case the impairment may be total, in the second one it may fall far below the requisite threshold.

Several tribunals have chosen to view the whole business enterprise as an investment, and not its constituent parts. These tribunals have denied the existence of an expropriation in cases where the investor was deprived of some rights but retained control over the overall investment.

For instance, the *Telenor Mobile v. Hungary* tribunal stated:

> *"The tribunal considers that, in the present case at least, the investment must be viewed as a whole and that the test the Tribunal has to apply is whether, viewed as a whole, the investment has suffered substantial erosion of value."*[38]

However, in certain cases, different interests belonging to the same business have been treated separately. Some tribunals have accepted that particular rights belonging to the same business may be expropriated without looking at the issue of control over the entire business (Dolzer and Schreuer, 2008, p. 108). The *EnCana v. Ecuador* arbitration discussed above illustrates that even such a discrete entitlement as a right to VAT refunds can be seen as an investment capable of being expropriated. In *Middle East Cement v. Egypt*,[39] the tribunal resolved, in separate analysis, whether an expropriation of the ship, the *Poseidon*, had occurred and whether the claimant's contractual rights had also been expropriated. Similarly, the *Waste Management v. Mexico* tribunal considered it appropriate to distinguish between a wholesale expropriation (the enterprise) and the expropriation of a particular asset (contractual rights) only.[40]

It is questionable whether an investor (or tribunal) may slice the relevant business into discrete elements in order to isolate one that has been most seriously impacted by the measure, especially in cases of indirect expropriation. If a shipping company has 30 vessels, a direct taking of even one of them does constitute an expropriation. However, an economic impact of a regulation that prohibits the exploitation of certain types of vessels due to their high levels of pollution (supposing 5 of out 30 vessels are affected by the regulation) may need to be assessed by reference to value of the shipping company as a whole.

The purpose of the definition of investment, which lists individual assets, is to define the general scope of the treaty application but, presumably, not to enable the individual treatment of those items or assets where they function as part of an integral business operation. It has been suggested that a partial expropriation can be found only if (a) the overall investment project can be disassembled into a number of discrete rights; (b) the State has deprived the investor of a right covered by the investment definition in the applicable treaty; and (c) the right is capable of economic exploitation independently of the remainder of the investment (Kriebaum, 2007a, p. 83). The last criterion is important, as it prevents an over-fragmentation of businesses into discrete pieces and allegations of expropriation with respect to such pieces. Under this approach, a right to tax refunds, goodwill or a market share may not be considered as individual investments that can be subject to expropriation.

3.   Contractual breaches versus expropriation of contracts

Tribunals have generally accepted that contractual rights may be expropriated. However, *"not every failure by a government to perform a contract amounts to an expropriation even if the violation leads to a loss of rights under the contract"* (Dolzer and Schreuer, 2008, p. 117). The mere breach by the State of a contract does not as such entail a breach of international law; likewise, a contractual breach does not in principle amount to an expropriation.

As pointed out in *Siemens v. Argentina, "for the behaviour of the State as party to a contract to be considered a breach of an investment treaty, such behaviour must be beyond that which an ordinary contracting party could adopt and involve State interference with the operation of the contract ..."*.[41]

More recently, in *Suez v. Argentina,* the tribunal reaffirmed that where the arbitration involves breaches of a contract concluded between a claimant and a host government,

> *"tribunals have made a distinction between* acta iure imperii *and* acta iure gestionis, *that is to say, actions by a State in exercise of its sovereign powers and actions of a State as a contracting party. It is the use by a State of its sovereign powers that gives rise to treaty breaches, while actions as a contracting party merely give rise to contract claims not ordinarily covered by an investment treaty."*[42]

To illustrate the foregoing, in *Azurix v. Argentina*, the tribunal had to determine whether the Argentine province of Buenos

Aires was acting in the exercise of its sovereign authority (as a political subdivision of the respondent) or as a party to a contract. The tribunal concluded that "*...the actions taken by the Province were taken in its capacity as a public authority and by issuing resolutions through its regulator and decrees, actions which can hardly be treated as those of 'a mere party to the contract'.*"[43] However, the claim of expropriation was dismissed on other grounds.

Another limitation with respect to claims regarding the expropriation of contractual rights is that the non-performance of a contractual obligation by a State or State entity does not necessarily amount to an expropriation. The tribunal in *Waste Management v. Mexico* clarified:

> "*The mere non-performance of a contractual obligation is not to be equated with a taking of property, nor (unless accompanied by other elements) is it tantamount to expropriation.... [T]he normal response by an investor faced with a breach of contract by its governmental counter-party (the breach not taking the form of an exercise of governmental prerogative, such as a legislative decree) is to sue in the appropriate court to remedy the breach. It is only where such access is legally or practically foreclosed that the breach could amount to a definitive denial of the right (i.e., the effective taking of the chose in action) and the protection of Article 1110 ['Expropriation'] be called into play.*"

In a similar vein, the tribunal in *SGS v. Philippines* held that:

> "*A mere refusal to pay a debt is not an expropriation of property, at least where remedies exist in respect of such a refusal. A fortiori a refusal to pay is not an expropriation where there is an unresolved dispute as to the amount payable*".[44]

This effectively means that an investor must first seek justice in the courts of the host State (if the contract so provides) and can raise an expropriation claim under an IIA only if the contractual remedies prove fruitless. There must be a definitive denial of the investor's contractual rights.

F. Requirements for a lawful expropriation

An overwhelming majority of IIAs allow States to expropriate investments as long as the taking is effected according to the following criteria:

(a) For a public purpose;
(b) In a non discriminatory manner;
(c) In accordance with due process of law;
(d) Against the payment of compensation.

IIAs may display some difference in formulations (as discussed below with respect to each condition) but in general, these four conditions have not changed or otherwise evolved in recent years (see recent examples in box 2). They have crystallized sufficiently to represent customary international law on expropriation.

Before analysing the conditions that determine the lawfulness of an expropriation, a tribunal should answer the question whether the expropriation has actually occurred. This is often a challenging task when the case involves an allegation of an indirect expropriation (relevant criteria are discussed in section II.A). It is important not to confuse the question whether there has been an expropriation with that of whether the conditions have been satisfied. Only after a tribunal concludes that the taking has indeed taken place, it should proceed to examine whether the four conditions have been met. Its analysis, in turn, will allow to conclude whether the expropriation was lawful or not.

Box 2. Recent examples of conditions for a lawful expropriation

Canada-Slovakia BIT (2010)

Article VI

"*1. Investments or returns of investors of either Contracting Party shall not be nationalized, expropriated or subjected to measures having an effect equivalent to nationalization or expropriation (hereinafter referred to as 'expropriation') in the territory of the other Contracting Party, except for a public purpose, under due process of law, in a non-discriminatory manner and provided that such expropriation is accompanied by prompt, adequate and effective compensation.*"

Netherlands-Oman BIT (2009)

Article 4

"*Neither Contracting Party shall take any measures depriving, directly or indirectly, nationals or persons of the other Contracting Party of their investments or measures having an equivalent effect unless the following conditions are complied with:*

(a) The measures are taken in the public interest and under due process of law;

(b) The measures are not discriminatory or contrary to any specific undertaking which the former Contracting Party may have given;

(c) The measures are accompanied by the provision for the payment of just compensation."

---

1.   Public purpose

The requirement that an expropriation must be made for a public purpose is recognized by most legal systems and is a rule of international law. The taking of property must be motivated by the pursuance of a legitimate welfare objective, as opposed to a purely private gain or an illicit end. This condition is reflected in most domestic legal systems as well, which indicates a convergence of approaches among States in various regions with different legal cultures.

IIAs generally refer to "public purpose", although some treaties use other formulations such as "public benefit" (Germany-Pakistan BIT (2009)), "public interest" (China-Peru FTA (2009)), "public order and social interest" (Canada-Colombia FTA (2008)), "internal needs" (Hong Kong, China-Thailand BIT (2006) and Israel-Slovakia BIT (2001)), "legal ends" (Malaysia-Uruguay BIT (1996)), "national interest" (Chile-Philippines BIT (1997) and Malaysia-United Arab Emirates BIT (1992)), "public necessity" (Peru-Singapore FTA (2008)) and "public purpose related to internal needs" (Angola-United Kingdom BIT (2000)).

Many of these formulations are equivalent in their scope and may be a result of different legal cultures and languages. However, some formulations may be interpreted as giving a narrower meaning to the requirement.

In any case, unless explicitly provided otherwise, the relevant terms will be read by arbitral tribunals by reference to their meaning under international law. Indeed, some recent treaties include clarifying footnotes indicating that public purpose refers to a concept of international law or customary international law. That is the case of the Peru-Singapore FTA (2008), which includes the following footnote:

> "*For greater certainty, for the purposes of this Article, public purpose refers to a concept in customary international law. Without prejudice to its definition under customary international law, public purpose may be similar or approximate to concepts under domestic law, for*

example, the concept of 'public necessity'. " (Article 10.10, footnote 10-9)

Similarly, the Canada-Colombia FTA (2008) includes the following footnote:

"The term 'public purpose' is a concept of public international law and shall be interpreted in accordance with international law. Domestic law may express this or similar concepts using different terms, such as 'social interest', 'public necessity' or 'public use'." (Article 811, footnote 7)

Perhaps the most significant variation used by some treaties is the reference to domestic law, which is meant to enable a tribunal to incorporate into its analysis the understanding of the relevant concept in domestic law. For instance, the Belgium/Luxembourg-Colombia BIT (2009) provides the following:

"It is understood that the criterion 'utilidad pública o interés social' contained in Article 58 of the Constitución Política de Colombia (1991) is compatible with the term 'public purpose' used in this Article." (Article IX(2))

In arbitral decisions, the notion of public purpose and the way it is used to assess the legality of an expropriation measure have been consistent over the last decade. It has been held that it is not enough to merely state that an expropriation is motivated by public purpose. In *ADC v. Hungary*, the tribunal noted that:

*"... **a treaty requirement for 'public interest' requires some genuine interest of the public**. If mere reference to 'public interest' can magically put such interest into existence and therefore satisfy this requirement, then this requirement would be rendered meaningless since the*

Tribunal can imagine no situation where this requirement would not have been met." [45] (Emphasis added.)

The public purpose requirement is considered by reference to the time when the expropriatory measure was taken. Whether or not the goal originally sought by the measure is achieved does not affect the public purpose requirement. Conversely, an expropriation that was effected but not for a public purpose will not be rendered lawful if the taken property starts serving a public purpose at a later stage.

In *Siag and Vecchi v. Egypt*, the Egyptian authorities expropriated the land owned by the claimants on grounds of delays in the construction of a tourist project. The measure did not contain an explicitly stated public policy objective. Six years after the date of the taking, the property was transferred to a public gas company for the construction of a pipeline. For the tribunal, the fact that the land was later used in a public-interest project was irrelevant:

"The Tribunal does not accept that because an investment was eventually put to public use, the expropriation of that investment must necessarily be said to have been 'for' a public purpose."[46]

Even though pursued for a public purpose, the direct expropriation, in order to be lawful under international law, must be accompanied by compensation to the investor. At the same time, when dealing with an allegation of an indirect (regulatory) expropriation, a broader assessment of the nature of the measure (which includes, but is not limited to, the public purpose) is essential in order to distinguish an indirect expropriation from the ordinary and legitimate regulatory conduct of the State, which is non-compensable (see subsection II.B).

The concept of public purpose is somewhat broad and abstract. International law has traditionally left it to each sovereign

State to decide for itself what it considers useful or necessary for the public good. The European Court of Human Rights has given States a wide margin of appreciation in this respect and has recognized that it is for national authorities to make the initial assessment of the existence of a public concern warranting measures that result in a dispossession (OECD, 2004, p. 17). In the case of *James and others v. United Kingdom*, the Court held that the State's judgement should be accepted unless exercised in a manifestly unreasonable way:

> *"The Court, finding it natural that the margin of appreciation available to the legislature in implementing social and economic policies should be a wide one, will respect the legislature's judgment as to what is 'in the public interest' unless that judgment be manifestly without reasonable foundation."*[47]

The specific motives are not considered important under international law, and international tribunals and courts have traditionally given strong deference to States as to whether an expropriation has been motivated by a public purpose. This issue has rarely been challenged and tribunals have tended to focus on other elements of legality. As noted in the Draft Convention on the International Responsibility of States for Injury to Aliens (1961),

> *"[t]his unwillingness to impose an international standard of public purpose must be taken as reflecting great hesitancy upon the part of tribunals and of States adjusting claims through diplomatic settlement to embark upon a survey of what the public needs of a nation are and how these may best be satisfied".*[48]

Nonetheless, in the context of investor-State disputes, tribunals have scrutinized the public purpose requirement in the past and seem keener to do so at present. In *BP Exploration Co. v. Libya*, the ad hoc arbitrator held that the taking of a foreign oil company as an act of political retaliation did not qualify as a public purpose. In that case, the reason for the expropriation was Libya's belief that the United Kingdom had encouraged Iran to occupy certain Persian Gulf islands. The tribunal concluded that the taking of the company's property, rights and interests *"violate[d] public international law as it was made for **purely extraneous political reasons** and was arbitrary and discriminatory in character"*.[49] (Emphasis added.)

By contrast, in the *Aminoil* arbitration the majority of the tribunal held that the oil company had been nationalized for a public purpose consistent with Kuwait's policy concerning its oil industry.[50]

In *ADC v. Hungary*, the tribunal found no public-interest justification. In the tribunal's view, the respondent failed to substantiate with convincing facts or legal reasoning that the expropriatory decree had been adopted for an alleged public purpose, namely the harmonization of the Hungarian legal regime with that of the European Union (EU).[51]

In *Siemens v. Argentina*, the dispute arose out of the termination of a contract for the provision of an integral service for the implementation of an immigration control, personal identification and electoral information system. The termination was carried out under the terms of the Emergency Law enacted in 2000 in response to an economic crisis, which empowered the President to renegotiate public-sector contracts. Although the tribunal showed deference as to the causes and objectives of the Emergency Law, it found no public purpose in a number of measures prior to the decree that terminated the contract as well as in the decree itself. It held that:

> *"...there* is no ***evidence of a public purpose in the measures prior to the issuance of Decree 669/01***. *It was an exercise of public authority to reduce the costs to Argentina of the Contract recently awarded through public competitive*

bidding, and as part of a change of policy by a new Administration eager to distance itself from its predecessor." (Emphasis added.)

"… while the public purpose of the 2000 Emergency Law is evident, its application through Decree 669/01 to the specific case of Siemens' investment and the public purpose of same are questionable."[52] (Emphasis added.)

In this case the tribunal appears to have ignored the high degree of deference to States that adjudicating bodies customarily have on this issue. Its decision can be seen as an example of an expansive approach to the condition of public purpose. Countries are the best judges of their own needs, values and circumstances, and tribunals should defer to their judgement unless there is evidence that the expropriation is manifestly without public purpose.

2.   Non-discrimination

IIAs generally impose the requirement that an expropriation be taken "on a non-discriminatory basis", "in a non-discriminatory manner" or "without discrimination". These variations in formulations are not legally significant.

Arbitral tribunals have found this requirement to have been violated when a State has discriminated against foreign nationals on the basis of their nationality. However, not all distinctions between different types or classes of investors are discriminatory (Newcombe and Paradell, 2009, p. 374). Tribunals take a nuanced approach to expropriations that affect only some foreigners if such discrimination may be the result of legitimate government policies (Reinisch, 2008, p. 186).

An expropriation that targets a foreign investor is not discriminatory per se: the expropriation must be based on, linked to or taken for reasons of, the investor's nationality. For instance, in

GAMI Investments v. Mexico, the Mexican government expropriated a number of sugar mills owned by a Mexican company with foreign participation. However, the expropriations were not taken because of the origin of the investments, but related instead to the precarious financial conditions of the expropriated mills. The tribunal held:

> "...*a reason exists for the measure which was not discriminatory. **That the measure plausibly connected with a legitimate goal of policy** (ensuring that the sugar industry was in the hands of solvent enterprises) and was applied neither in a discriminatory manner nor as a disguised barrier to equal opportunity.*
>
> ...***GAMI*** [the foreign investor] ***has failed to demonstrate that the measure it invokes resulted from or have any connection with GAMI's participation in GAM*** [the local company which owned the mills]*; nor were they geared towards treating GAM in a different mode because of GAMI's participation in their social capital.*"[53] (Emphasis added.)

In *ADC v. Hungary*, the tribunal did not accept the respondent's argument that claimants were not in a position to raise any claims of being treated discriminately as they were the only foreign parties involved in the operation of the airport. The tribunal agreed that "*in order for a discrimination to exist, particularly in an expropriation scenario, there must be different treatments to different parties*".[54] Although the claimants were the only foreign parties affected by the measures, the tribunal found that the treatment received by the operator appointed by Hungary and that received by foreign investors as a whole was different and thus discriminatory.[55]

In *Eureko v. Poland*, the dispute arose out of a privatization of an insurance company. The claimant had purchased 30 per cent of the shares and later acquired a right to purchase a further 21 per cent equity through an addendum to the initial agreement. Having found that the frustration of the right to acquire further shares constituted an expropriation, the tribunal considered the issue of discrimination:

> "*...the measures taken by [Poland] in refusing to conduct the IPO [purchase of additional shares] are clearly discriminatory. As the Tribunal noted earlier, these measures have been proclaimed by successive Ministers of the State Treasury as being pursued in order to keep PZU [the privatized State-owned insurance company] under majority Polish control and to exclude foreign control such as that of Eureko. That discriminatory conduct by the Polish Government is blunt violation of the expectations of the Parties in concluding the SPA [Share Purchase Agreement] and the First Addendum*."[56] (Emphasis added.)

Thus, the tribunal found that the State mistreated the claimant because of its foreign origin and held that such treatment was discriminatory.

3.   Due process of law

The due-process principle requires (a) that the expropriation comply with procedures established in domestic legislation and fundamental internationally recognized rules in this regard and (b) that the affected investor have an opportunity to have the case reviewed before an independent and impartial body (right to an independent review).

In addition, the expropriation process must be free from arbitrariness. The International Court of Justice (ICJ) defined arbitrariness as "*a wilful disregard of due process of law, an act which shocks, or at least surprises, a sense of juridical propriety*".[57]

Examples of disregard of due process would be when an expropriation lacks legal basis (no law or procedure properly established beforehand to order the expropriation), when the investor has no recourse to domestic courts or administrative tribunals in order to challenge the measure or when the State engages in abusive conduct.

Treaty wording can have significant implications when it comes to assessing the requirement. However, whether explicitly referred to or not, the relevant procedures must be assessed against the domestic laws and regulations of the host State and its judicial and administrative system.

Most IIAs include a reference to due process of law as a condition for an expropriation to be lawful. This is the case in treaties such as NAFTA, the Energy Charter Treaty, the ASEAN Comprehensive Investment Agreement and many recent FTAs and BITs. The most significant variation to that formula is the reference to "legal provisions" (China-Costa Rica BIT (1999), Republic of Korea-Nigeria BIT (1997)), "legal procedures" (Republic of Korea-Mexico BIT (2000), China-Côte d'Ivoire BIT (2002), China-Djibouti (2003)), "legality" (Argentina-Mexico BIT (1996)) or other formulations explicitly referring to the domestic law of the host State as a standard of due process. This is also the case of the Oman-Switzerland BIT (2009) which states:

> "*Neither of the Contracting Parties shall take measures of expropriation ... unless ... such measures are taken on a non-discriminatory basis and in **accordance with domestic laws of general application**. The legality of any such expropriation and the amount of compensation shall at the request of the investor be subject to review by due process of law.*" (Emphasis added.)

Some IIAs specifically set out the requirement that a measure be subject to recourse or review, as for example the Serbia and Montenegro-Switzerland BIT (2005), which states:

"*The investor affected by the expropriation shall have a right, under the law of the Contracting Party making the expropriation,* **to prompt review, by a judicial or other independent authority of that Contracting Party**, *of his case and of the valuation of his investment in accordance with the principles set out in this Article.*" (Article XX, emphasis added.)

The Austria-Mexico BIT (1998) contains a similar formulation:

"*Due process of law includes the right of an investor of a Contracting Party which claims to be affected by expropriation by the other Contracting Party to prompt review of its case, including the valuation of its investment and the payment of compensation in accordance with the provisions of this Article, by a judicial authority or another competent and independent authority of the latter Contracting Party.*" (Article 4(3))

Compliance with the due-process requirement has been reviewed by some arbitral tribunals. In *Middle East Cement v. Egypt*, a vessel used by the investor to conduct its business operation had been seized and was later auctioned by the port authorities. The tribunal determined that these acts did not meet the requirement for due process, given the irregularities identified with respect to the notification process:

"*...**a matter as important as the seizure and auctioning of a ship of the Claimant should have been notified by a direct communication** for which the law No. 308 provided under the 1st paragraph of Art. 7, irrespective of whether there was a legal duty or practice to do so by registered mail with return receipt requested as argued by Claimant (CV 4). The Tribunal finds that the procedure in fact applied here does not fulfil the requirements of Art. 2.2 [fair and* *equitable treatment] and 4 [expropriation] of the BIT.*"[58] (Emphasis added.)

In *ADC v. Hungary*, the tribunal found a violation of the requirement for due process, and stated as follows:

"...'*due process of law*', *in the expropriation context, demands an actual and substantive legal procedure for a foreign investor to raise its claims against the depriving actions already taken or about to be taken against it. Some basic legal mechanisms, such as reasonable advance notice, a fair hearing and an unbiased and impartial adjudicator to assess the actions in dispute, are expected to be readily available and accessible to the investor to make such legal procedure meaningful. In general, the legal procedure must be of a nature to grant an affected investor a reasonable chance within a reasonable time to claim its legitimate rights and have its claims heard. If no legal procedure of such nature exists at all, the argument that 'the actions are taken under due process of law' rings hollow.*"[59] (Emphasis added.)

More recently, in *Siag & Vecchi v. Egypt*, the tribunal found that due process had been denied both substantially and procedurally. It held that claimants, under the BIT between Egypt and Italy, suffered a denial of substantive due process because their contract was cancelled, and their investment expropriated, without a valid reason some seven months before a fixed deadline for completing Phase One of the project. [60] Moreover, the claimants "...*ought to have received notice that the [Touristic Development Agency] was considering expropriating the investment. Claimants received no such notice and were not afforded the opportunity, until after the fact, to be heard on the matter*". The tribunal found that the failure by Egypt to provide such notice constituted a procedural abuse.[61]

The need to give a prior notice of the expropriation as part of the due process requirement is not well established. Prior notice is not necessarily a requirement, especially when an expropriation measure is taken in circumstances of imminent necessity or emergency. The due-process requirement should be deemed fulfilled as long the expropriation is carried out in accordance with the domestic law, in a non-arbitrary manner and with an opportunity for the investor to have the measure reviewed.

4.   Payment of compensation

The last condition for an expropriation to be lawful is that it must be accompanied by compensation. Different methods of valuation may be employed to determine the amount of compensation (see sections I.F.4(iv) and III.B) and may lead to varying results. The differences between compensation for lawful expropriation and reparation for unlawful expropriation are discussed separately in section III.A.

In recent IIAs, there is an increasing level of convergence regarding the standard of compensation that must be paid to render the expropriation lawful. One of the salient trends among IIAs is that most of them incorporate the standard of prompt, adequate and effective compensation, also known as the Hull standard (see UNCTAD, 2007, p. 48).

Compensation is considered to be prompt if paid without delay; adequate, if it has a reasonable relationship with the market value of the investment concerned; and effective, if paid in convertible or freely useable currency.

In spelling out what constitutes an adequate compensation, treaties most often refer to an investment's fair market value. One can also encounter references to market value, just price, real value, genuine value or real economic value (see box 3). While some of the formulas may achieve the same effect, others give more or less flexibility to arbitral tribunals in the evaluation of the compensation. In several cases, some of these formulations have been deemed to be equivalent to the fair market value concept.[62] The World Bank Guidelines on the Treatment of Foreign Direct Investment define fair market value as:

> "*An amount that a willing buyer would normally pay to a willing seller* after taking into account the nature of the investment, the circumstances in which it would operate in the future and its specific characteristics, including the period in which it has been in existence, the proportion of tangible assets in the total investment and other relevant factors pertinent to the specific circumstances of each case."[63] (Emphasis added.)

Full compensation equal to the market value of the property is not the only possible standard of compensation. The standard widely discussed in the 1960s and 1970s is that of "appropriate" compensation, which is embodied in United Nations General Assembly resolutions[64] and may still represent the standard of customary international law. Under some interpretations, this standard justifies less than full compensation where this is fair in the circumstances of the case.[65] Some IIAs use standards that refer to fairness and equity, which arguably gives more room for balancing private and public interests (e.g. "just" compensation in the Chile-Tunisia BIT (1998), "fair and equitable" compensation in the India-United Kingdom BIT (1994) or "just and equitable" compensation in the Mozambique-Netherlands BIT (2001)). The Charter of Fundamental Rights of the European Union (2000) requires payment of "fair" compensation; in the practice of the European Court of Human Rights, compensation for a lawful expropriation of property must be "reasonably related to its value", even though "legitimate objectives of 'public interest' may call for less than reimbursement of the full market value".[66]

Box 3. Different approaches as regards compensation	
Fair market value	**Genuine value**
ASEAN Comprehensive Investment Agreement (2009) Article 14 "[…] *2. The compensation referred to in sub-paragraph 1(c) shall:* *(a) be paid without delay;* *(b) be equivalent to the* **fair market value** *of the expropriated investment immediately before or at the time when the expropriation was publicly announced, or when the expropriation occurred, whichever is applicable;[…]"* (Emphasis added.)	**Netherlands-Oman BIT (2009)** Article 4 "[…] *c) …Such compensation shall represent the* **genuine value** *of the investments affected immediately before the date the measures or impending measures became public knowledge and shall, in order to be effective for the claimants, be paid and made transferable, without undue delay, to the country designated by the claimants concerned and in the currency of the country of which the claimants are nationals or persons or in any freely convertible currency accepted by the claimants."* (Emphasis added.)
Just compensation	**Real value**
Chile-Tunisia BIT (1998) Article 6 *"(1) Neither Contracting Party shall nationalize, expropriate or subject the investments of an investor of the other Contracting Party to any measures having an*	**Slovenia-Turkey BIT (2004)** Article 4 "[…] *2. Such compensation shall amount to the* **real value** *of the expropriated investment at the expropriated investment at the* /…

Box 3. Different approaches as regards compensation (concluded)	
equivalent effect (hereinafter referred to as 'expropriation') unless the following conditions are complied with: [...] *(2) The measures are taken against just compensation."* (Emphasis added.)	*time immediately before the expropriatory action was taken or became known."* (Emphasis added.)

An important issue is whether the non-payment of compensation renders unlawful a measure that meets the other three conditions, or whether this only provides the basis for a claim to compensation.

Some commentators observe that numerous awards of the Iran-United States Claims Tribunal *"recognize the payment of prompt compensation to be a consideration relevant to the lawfulness of a taking under customary international law"* (Brower and Brueschke, 1998, p. 499). Some arbitral awards rendered in IIA cases suggest that non-payment of compensation renders the expropriation unlawful.[67]

This approach is questionable. The payment of compensation is a remedy available in case of a dispute and can be awarded by an arbitral tribunal. Particularly in determining the existence of an indirect expropriation and assessing a regulatory measure, the tribunal needs to first characterize the measure before looking into the existence of a duty to pay compensation. When the expropriatory nature of the measure is being opposed, it cannot be expected that the host State makes a pre-emptive payment.

In this regard, a distinction has been drawn between expropriations which are unlawful *sub modo*, i.e. that would be lawful if compensation was paid, and expropriations which are unlawful per se, i.e. that breach other conditions of lawfulness such as public purpose or non-discrimination (Brownlie, 2008, p. 538). Some have argued that *"[n]on-payment of compensation does not make an otherwise lawful nationalization unlawful"* (Sornarajah, 2004, p. 345). In *Santa Elena v. Costa Rica*[68] and *SPP v. Egypt*,[69] where legitimate takings only lacking compensation were at stake, the tribunals never referred to the expropriations as unlawful.

The European Court of Human Rights distinguishes between inherent illegality of a taking, for example a taking that is not in the public interest, and illegality due to the non-payment of compensation. Only inherently illegal expropriations trigger automatic application of a higher compensation standard. Thus, in the practice of the European Court, even though the non-payment of compensation is wrongful, it does not trigger the same consequences that follow from an inherently illegal taking.[70]

Indeed, an act of expropriation meeting the requirements set forth in international law constitutes a lawful act of the State, and the duty to pay compensation is the consequence of the legal exercise of a recognized sovereign right of a State. This requirement may be met from the outset or after litigation, when the expropriatory nature of the act is established.

While failure by a State to pay any compensation for a direct expropriation can be seen as rendering such an expropriation unlawful, this should not be the case when a measure at stake allegedly constitutes an indirect expropriation. Even if the measure is found by a tribunal to be expropriatory, the obligation to pay compensation should arise only as a consequence of such finding.

4.1   Applicable interest

Many older IIAs do not address the issue of applicable interest. The trend in recent treaty practice has been to explicitly provide for the payment of interest from the date of the taking until the date of payment.

Most recent treaties contain guidelines on the applicable rate of interest (see examples in box 4) and do so in a variety of ways, some of which are rather vague (e.g. "appropriate", "fair", "commercially reasonable" interest) while others are quite precise (e.g. LIBOR rate – acronym for London Interbank Offered Rate[71]).

Box 4. Interest rate	
Appropriate interest	**Japan-Philippines Economic Partnership Agreement (2006)** Article 95 "...*The compensation shall be paid without delay and shall carry an **appropriate interest**, taking into account the length of time from the time of expropriation until the time of payment.*" (Emphasis added.)
Commercially reasonable interest	**Agreement for the COMESA Common Investment Area (2007)** Article 20 " [...] *3. If payment is made in a currency of the host or home State, compensation shall include interest at a **commercially reasonable rate** for that currency from the date of expropriation until the date of actual payment.*" (Emphasis added.)
LIBOR rate	**Brunei-Republic of Korea BIT (2000)** Article 5 "...*shall include interest at the applicable commercial rate or **LIBOR rate**, whichever is higher, from the date of expropriation until the date of payment and....*" (Emphasis added.) /...

	Box 4. (continued)
	Finland-Viet Nam BIT (2008) Article 4 "*2. ...The compensation shall **include interest at the rate of London Interbank Offered Rate (LIBOR) for three-month deposits in the respective currency** from the date of expropriation or loss until the date of payment.*" (Emphasis added.)
Commercially applicable rate as set by the national bank of the expropriating Party	**Panama-Taiwan Province of China FTA (2003)** Article 10.11 "*4. ...The compensation shall include the payment of interests computed from the day of dispossession of the expropriated investment until the day of payment, and shall be computed on the basis of a **commercially applicable rate for this currency set by the national bank system of the Party** where the expropriation occurred.*" (Emphasis added.)
Rate prevailing in the banking system	**Czech Republic-Republic of Moldova BIT (1999)** Article 5 "*1. ... Interest based on the **average deposit rate prevailing in the national banking system** from the date of expropriation ....*" (Emphasis added.)
Domestic law of the expropriating Party	**Hong Kong, China-Thailand (2005)** Article 5 "*1. ...such compensation ... shall include **interest at the rate applicable under the law of the Contracting Party making the deprivation** until the date of payment....*" (Emphasis added.)

/...

Box 4. (concluded)	
Fair and equitable rate	**India-Mozambique BIT (2009)** Article 5 "1. *...shall include interest at a **fair and equitable rate** until the date of payment....*" (Emphasis added.)
Normal market rate	**India-Latvia BIT (2010)** Article 5 "1. *...shall include interest at the **normal market rate** until the date of payment, shall be made without unreasonable delay, be effectively realizable and be freely transferable.*" (Emphasis added.)
Usual commercial rate	**Oman-Switzerland BIT (2009)** Article 6 "*...The amount of compensation shall carry **the usual commercial interest** from the date of dispossession until payment....*" (Emphasis added.)

Some treaties lay down the obligation to pay interest only in those situations when the payment of the principal amount of compensation is delayed. For instance, the Romania-Turkey BIT (1991) provides that "*in the event that payment of compensation is delayed, the investor shall receive interest for the period of any **undue delay** in making payment*" (Article 4(2), emphasis added). It is worth highlighting that IIAs generally do not specify whether interest should be simple or compound. Tribunals have dealt with this issue on a case-by-case basis and have generally favoured compound interest. This approach aims to compensate investors in full and is more costly for defendant States. The fairness of this approach is questionable in cases involving indirect expropriations where the characterization of a measure as expropriatory is often disputed by the State, and the duty to pay compensation arises as a result of an arbitral decision.

4.2   Currency of payment

Some IIAs, particularly those concluded before 2000, do not specify the currency to be used for purposes of the payment of compensation.[72] The predominant current trend is to provide that compensation must be paid in a "freely convertible currency". For example, the Ethiopia-Spain BIT (2006) provides that the market value of the expropriated investment *"shall be expressed in a freely convertible currency at the market exchange rate of exchange prevailing for that currency on the valuation date"* (Article 5(3), emphasis added). A freely convertible currency can be immediately converted into other currencies on the foreign exchange market.

Other agreements, such as the Australia-Egypt BIT (2001), provide that compensation may be paid in the currency in which the investment was originally made, or, at the request of the investor, in any other freely convertible currency (Article 7(3)). The Japan-Philippines EPA (2006) provides that the compensation shall be convertible *"into the currency of the Party of the investors concerned and freely usable currencies defined in the Articles of Agreement of the International Monetary Fund"* (Article 95(3)).

4.3   Period of payment

Most IIAs provide that payment must be "prompt", "without delay" or "without undue delay". For instance, the BIT between Japan and Lao People's Democratic Republic BIT (2008) provides that *"compensation shall be paid without delay..."* (Article 12(3)). This approach grants some flexibility to the host State. The timeframe should be assessed in light of the specific experience of each State and the normal procedures in place to make an effective payment. In many countries, a normal time to make such transfer would be between three and six months.

However, there may be exceptional cases where a State faces circumstances such as foreign exchange restrictions or constraints. In this case, for example, the 1992 World Bank Guidelines on the Treatment of Foreign Direct Investment recommend that compensation be paid in instalments within a period that *"will be as short as possible and which will not in any case exceed five years from the time of the taking, provided that reasonable, market-related interest applies to the deferred payments in the same currency"*. (Guideline IV.8)

Some treaties lay down a specific period of time within which the payment of compensation must be made. For instance, the Croatia-Czech Republic BIT (2008) provides that:

> *"A transfer shall be deemed to be made 'without undue delay' if effected within such period as is normally required for the completion or transfer formalities. **The said period shall commence on the day on which the relevant request has been submitted and may not exceed three months.**"* (Article 4(2), emphasis added.)

4.4   Methods of valuation

Some treaties refer to the methods of valuation to be used or considered in order to assess the value of an expropriated investment. For instance, NAFTA (1992) provides that *"valuation criteria shall include going concern value, asset value including declared tax value of tangible property, and other criteria, as appropriate, to determine fair market value"* (Article 1110(2)). The same approach has been followed by the Republic of Korea-Mexico BIT (2000), the Canada-Peru BIT (2006) and other treaties. Some IIAs require that the value of an investment be determined *"in accordance with generally recognized principles of valuation"* (e.g.

the China-Côte d'Ivoire BIT (2002)). The Oman-Switzerland BIT (2004) also refers to recognized principles of valuation, but supplements this with an illustrative list of methods and factors (different from those in NAFTA) that can be taken into account:

> "*[t]he compensation ... shall be equivalent to the fair market value of the investment, as determined in accordance with recognized principles of valuation such as, inter alia, the capital invested, replacement value, appreciation, current returns, goodwill and other relevant factors...*" (Article 6(2)).

These formulations provide a useful indication but ultimately leave the choice of an appropriate valuation method to arbitrators.

Some treaties additionally mention equitable principles. Such a reference would seem to give arbitrators a mandate to grant compensation that they deem fair in the circumstances, and makes the connection between the amount of compensation and the market value of the investment less rigid. For instance, the Australia-Thailand FTA (2004) provides that:

> "*where [the] value cannot be readily ascertained, the compensation shall be determined in accordance with generally recognized principles of valuation and equitable principles taking into account, where appropriate, the capital invested, depreciation, capital already repatriated, replacement value, currency exchange rate movements and other relevant factors*" (Article 912(2)).

Similar formulations can be found in Chile's BITs with the Philippines (1995) and South Africa (1998).

The Costa Rica- Taiwan Province of China BIT (1999) appears to go further by providing, in a Protocol, that the valuation shall only take into account "real and permanent damages", excluding "future events", "expectations" and "capital gains" (box 5). Although the clarity of the provision could be improved, one possible reading is that it rules out compensation for future profits, and – by implication – the use of the discounted cash flow (DCF) valuation method (on DCF valuation, see section III.B). The exclusion of the DCF method means that in many cases the amount of compensation will be lower than it would be if that method were applied.

Box 5. Limitation of compensation in the

Costa Rica- Taiwan Province of China BIT (1999)

Protocol - Ad Article V

"For purposes of Article V, paragraph 2, the Contracting Parties agree that the concept of fair market price will be equal to the amount of compensation to be determined as follows:

[...]

The valuations shall take into account only real permanent damage. Future events or legal expectations of entitlement that affect the property shall not be included or taken into account. Capital gains resulting from the expropriation shall not be recognized either." (Unofficial translation)

---

5.   Additional requirements under IIAs

Some treaties add further conditions to assess the legality of an expropriation. For instance, the Bangladesh-United States BIT (1986) provides that the expropriation shall not *"violate any specific provision on contractual stability"* (Article 3(1)(d)). Similarly, the Netherlands-Oman BIT (2009) sets forth that the expropriatory measures shall not be *"discriminatory or contrary to any specific undertaking which the former Contracting Party may have given"* (Article 4(b)). The Belgium/Luxembourg-Colombia BIT (2009) provides that the *"measures shall be taken in a non-discriminatory manner, in good faith ..."* (Article IX(1)(b)).

Notes

[1]   *Case concerning certain German interests in Polish Upper Silesia (The Merits), Germany v. Poland*, Permanent Court of International Justice, Judgment, 25 May 1925. Full case references are provided in the References section.

[2]   *Norwegian Shipowners' Claims, Norway v. the United States*, Permanent Court of Arbitration, Award, 13 October 1922.

[3]   *Starrett Housing v. Iran*, Interlocutory Award No. ITL 32-24-1, 19 December 1983, 4 Iran-United States Claims Tribunal Reports 122, p. 154.

[4]   Unless indicated otherwise, the texts of IIAs mentioned in the paper can be found in the UNCTAD databases at www.unctad.org/iia.

[5]   *Generation Ukraine v. Ukraine*, Award, 16 September 2003, para. 20.22.

[6]   *Suez et al. v. Argentina*, Decision on Liability, 30 July 2010, para. 121.

[7]   Article 6.2.c of the Colombia-India BIT (2009).

[8]   Annex B.13 of the Canada-Jordan BIT (2009).

[9]   Annex B.13 of the Canada-Peru BIT (2006).

[10] Annex A of the Canada-Slovak Republic BIT (2010).

[11] Annex 11-B of the Australia-United States FTA (2004).

[12] Annex 10-C of CAFTA-DR.

[13] Annex 10-D of the Chile-United States FTA (2003).

[14] Annex 10-B of the Morocco-United States FTA (2004).

[15] Annex 9 of the China-Peru FTA (2009).

[16] Article 20.8 of the Investment Agreement for the COMESA Common Investment Area (2007).

[17] Article 5 of the Turkey model BIT.

[18] *Saluka v. Czech Republic*, Partial Award, 17 March 2006, para. 255.

[19] *Methanex v. USA, Final Award*, 3 August 2005, part IV, chapter D, para. 7.

[20] International Law Commission Articles on Responsibility of States for Internationally Wrongful Acts, 2001, Article 4.

[21] See, for example, *EDF v. Romania*, Award, 8 October 2009; *Hamester v. Ghana*, Award, 18 June 2010; *Jan de Nul v. Egypt*, Award, 6 November 2008 and other cases.

[22] See *Starrett Housing v. Iran*, Interlocutory Award No. ITL 32-24-1, 19 December 1983; *Tippetts, Abbett, McCarthy, Stratton v. Iran et al.*, Award No. 141-7-2, 19 June 1984.

[23] *Occidental v. Ecuador*, Award, 1 July 2004, para. 85.

[24] *EnCana v. Ecuador*, Award, 3 February 2006.

[25] Ibid., paras. 179–183.

[26] *Amoco v. Iran,* Award No. 310-56-3, 14 July 1987, para. 108.

[27] *Pope & Talbot v. Canada*, Interim Award, 26 June 2000, para. 96.

[28] *Methanex v. USA*, Final Award, 3 August 2005, Part IV, Chapter D, para. 17.

[29] *Chemtura v. Canada*, Award, 2 August 2010, para. 258.

[30] *Phillips Petroleum v. Iran*, Award No. 425-39-2, 29 June 1989, para. 76.

[31] *Starrett Housing v. Iran*, Interlocutory Award No. ITL 32-24-1, 19 December 1983, 4 Iran-United States Claims Tribunal Reports 122, p.156.

[32] See, for example, *Wena Hotels v. Egypt*, Award, 8 December 2000, para. 98 (expropriation is not limited to tangible property rights); *SPP v. Egypt,* Award, 20 May 1992, para. 164 (taking of contractual rights involves an obligation to pay compensation therefor); *SD Myers v. Canada*, Partial Award, 13 November 2000, para. 281 ("in legal theory, rights other than property rights may be expropriated"); *Bayindir v. Pakistan*, Award, 27 August 2009, para. 255 (expropriation "is not limited to in rem rights and may extend to contractual rights"); *Methanex v. USA*, Final Award, 3 August 2005, Part IV, Chapter D, para. 17 ("the restrictive notion of property as a material 'thing' is obsolete and has ceded its place to a contemporary conception which includes managerial control over components of a process that is wealth producing").

[33] *GAMI Investments v. Mexico*, Final Award, 15 November 2004, para. 123.

[34] Ibid., para. 127.

35 *Suez et al. v. Argentina*, Decision on Liability, 30 July 2010, para. 140.
36 *EnCana v. Ecuador*, Award, 3 February 2006, para. 184.
37 *Enron v. Argentina*, Decision on Jurisdiction, 14 January 2004, para. 70.
38 *Telenor v. Hungary*, Award, 13 September 2006, para 67.
39 *Middle East Cement v. Egypt*, Award, 12 April 2002.
40 *Waste Management v. Mexico*, Final Award, 30 April 2004, paras. 141 and 155.
41 *Siemens v. Argentina*, Award, 6 February 2007, para. 248.
42 *Suez et al. v. Argentina*, Decision on Liability, 30 July 2010, para. 142. See also *Consortium R.F.C.C. v. Morocco*, Award, 22 December 2003, para. 65 (a breach of a contract will not amount to expropriation "unless it be proved that the State or its emanation has gone beyond its role as a mere party to the contract, and has exercised the specific functions of a sovereign"), quoted with approval in *Azurix v. Argentina*, Award, 14 July 2006, para. 315.
43 *Azurix v. Argentina*, Award, 14 July 2006, para. 53.
44 *SGS v. Philippines*, Decision on Jurisdiction, 29 January 2004, para. 161.
45 *ADC v. Hungary*, Award, 2 October 2006, para. 432.
46 *Siag and Vecchi v. Egypt*, Award, 1 June 2009, para. 432.
47 *James and others v. United Kingdom*, European Court of Human Rights, Judgement, 21 February 1986, para. 46. Also, *Pressos Compania Naviera S.A. and others v. Belgium*, Judgement, 20 November 1995, para. 37.
48 Draft Convention on the International Responsibility of States for Injury to Aliens (1961), explanatory note to article 10.
49 *BP v. Libya*, Award, 10 October 1973, 53 ILR 297 (1979), p. 329.
50 *Government of Kuwait v. American Independent Oil Company (AMINOIL)*, Award, 24 March 1982, para. 85.
51 *ADC v. Hungary*, Award, 2 October 2006, para. 429.
52 *Siemens v. Argentina*, Award, 6 February 2007, para. 273.
53 *GAMI Investments v. Mexico*, Award, 15 November 2004, paras. 114–115.
54 *ADC v. Hungary*, Award, 2 October 2006, para. 442.
55 Ibid., para. 443.
56 *Eureko v. Poland*, Partial Award, 19 August 2005, para.242.

[57] *Elettronica Sicila S.p.A. (ELSI) v. United States of America,* International Court of Justice, Judgment, 20 July 1989, para. 128.

[58] *Middle East Cement v. Egypt,* Award, 12 April 2002, para. 143.

[59] *ADC v. Hungary,* Award, 2 October 2006, para. 435.

[60] *Siag and Vecchi v. Egypt,* Award, 1 June 2009, para. 441.

[61] Ibid., para. 442.

[62] *Vivendi v. Argentina II,* Award, 20 August 2007, para. 8.2.10; *Siemens v. Argentina,* Award, 6 February 2007, para. 353.

[63] Article IV.5 of the World Bank Guidelines on the Treatment of Foreign Direct Investment.

[64] Resolution 1803 (XVII), 14 December 1962, Declaration on Permanent Sovereignty over Natural Resources, para. 4; Resolution 3281 (XXIX), 12 December 1974, The Charter of Economic Rights and Duties of States (A/RES/29/3281), Article 2(c).

[65] See Lauterpacht, 1990, p. 249.

[66] *Pincova and Pinc v. the Czech Republic,* European Court of Human Rights, Judgment, 5 November 2002, para. 53.

[67] For example, *Vivendi v. Argentina II,* Award, 20 August 2007, para. 7.5.21; *Siemens v. Argentina,* Award, 6 February 2007, paras. 259, 273; *ADC v. Hungary,* Final Award, 2 October 2006, paras. 398 and 444.

[68] *Santa Elena. v. Costa Rica,* Award, 17 February 2000.

[69] *SPP v. Egypt,* Award, 20 May 1992.

[70] E.g. *Former King of Greece v. Greece,* Article 41 Judgment, 28 November 2002, para. 78. See also *Yagtzilar and Others v. Greece* Article 41 Judgment, 15 January 2004, para. 25; *Scordino v. Italy (No. 1),* Judgment, 29 March 2006, para. 255.

[71] A daily reference rate based on the interest rates at which banks borrow unsecured funds from other banks in the London wholesale money market or interbank lending market.

[72] See, for example, Pakistan-Syria BIT (1996), South Africa-Turkey BIT (2000), Germany-Sri Lanka BIT (2000) and Mauritius-South Africa BIT (1998).

II. ESTABLISHING AN INDIRECT EXPROPRIATION AND DISTINGUISHING IT FROM NON-COMPENSABLE REGULATION

The matter of establishing an indirect expropriation without impeding the right of States to regulate in the public interest has been one of the more challenging problems in recent years. This section aims to review the relevant treaty and arbitral practice and contribute to the development of an appropriate analytical framework.

Section A examines the factors used to evaluate whether an indirect expropriation has occurred. These include assessing the impact on the investment, interference with investor's legitimate expectations and the characteristics of the measure at stake.

Section B discusses how IIAs have singled out non-compensable regulatory measures and distinguishes them from cases of indirect expropriation. Such measures do not require compensation even where they produce a significant negative effect on an investment.

Section C concludes the preceding discussion by providing a framework for analysis of whether a certain governmental measure constitutes an indirect expropriation.

A.   Establishing an indirect expropriation

The most important development in treaty practice as regards expropriation is the inclusion of detailed provisions concerning indirect expropriation. Many recent treaties have taken this approach to clarify the relevant factors since there is no uniform definition of what measure constitutes an indirect expropriation. They generally require a case-by-case, fact-based inquiry and list several relevant factors that need to be considered in order to decide whether or not a measure constitutes an indirect expropriation.

In 2004, Canada and the United States became the first countries to incorporate a relevant Annex in their model BITs (see box 6).

Box 6. United States and Canadian model provisions on indirect expropriation	
United States Model BIT (2004) Annex B Expropriation	**Canadian Model BIT (2004)** Annex B.13(1) Expropriation
"The Parties confirm their shared understanding that: *1. Article 6 (1) [Expropriation and Compensation] is intended to reflect customary international law concerning the obligation of States with respect to expropriation.* *2. An action or a series of actions by a Party cannot constitute an expropriation unless it interferes with a tangible or intangible property right or property interest in an investment.* *3. Article 6 (1) addresses two situations. The first is direct expropriation, where an investment is nationalized or otherwise directly expropriated through formal transfer of title or outright seizure.* *4. The second situation addressed by Article 6 (1) is indirect expropriation, where an action or series of actions by a Party has an*	*"The Parties confirm their shared understanding that:* *a) Indirect expropriation results from a measure or series of measures of a Party that have an effect equivalent to direct expropriation without formal transfer of title or outright seizure;* *b) The determination of whether a measure or series of measures of a Party constitute an indirect expropriation requires a case-by-case, fact-based inquiry that considers, among other factors:* *(i) The economic impact of the measure or series of measures, although the sole fact that a measure or series of measures of a Party has an adverse effect on the economic*
	/...

Box 6. (concluded)	
effect equivalent to direct expropriation without formal transfer of title or outright seizure. *(a) The determination of whether an action or series of actions by a Party, in a specific fact situation, constitutes an indirect expropriation, requires a case-by-case, fact-based inquiry that considers, among other factors:* *(i) The economic impact of the government action, although the fact that an action or series of actions by a Party has an adverse effect on the economic value of an investment, standing alone, does not establish that an indirect expropriation has occurred;* *(ii) The extent to which the government action interferes with distinct, reasonable investment-backed expectations; and* *(iii) The character of the government action.* *(b) Except in rare circumstances, non-discriminatory regulatory actions by a Party that are designed and applied to protect legitimate public welfare objectives, such as public health, safety, and the environment, do not constitute indirect expropriations."*	*value of an investment does not establish that an indirect expropriation has occurred;* *(ii) The extent to which the measure or series of measures interfere with distinct, reasonable investment-backed expectations; and* *(iii) The character of the measure or series of measures;* *c) Except in rare circumstances, such as when a measure or series of measures are so severe in the light of their purpose that they cannot be reasonably viewed as having been adopted and applied in good faith, non-discriminatory measures of a Party that are designed and applied to protect legitimate public welfare objectives, such as health, safety and the environment, do not constitute indirect expropriation."*

Since 2004, both the United States and Canada have been including such an annex in their FTAs and BITs – see, for example, the United States' FTAs with Australia (2004), CAFTA-DR (2004), Morocco (2004) and Peru (2006); the Rwanda-United States BIT (2008); and Canada's BITs with Peru (2007), Romania (2009), Latvia (2009), Jordan (2009) and the Czech Republic (2009). Similar rules (in the form of an annex or incorporated into the expropriation provision itself) can be found in IIAs entered into by other countries, for instance, Australia-Chile (2008), India-Republic of Korea (2009), China-New Zealand (2008), Japan-Peru (2008), Belgium/Luxembourg-Colombia (2009) and Singapore-Peru (2009).

Most provisions on indirect expropriation found in recent FTAs and BITs are based on the United States and Canadian BIT models of 2004. There are however variations. For instance, the Annex on Expropriation in the China-New Zealand FTA (2008), includes additional criteria for assessing State conduct, including proportionality, discrimination and breach of the State's previous written commitments to the investor (see box 7).

Box 7. China-New Zealand FTA (2008)

Annex 13: Expropriation

"1. An action or a series of actions by a Party cannot constitute an expropriation unless it interferes with a tangible or intangible property right or property interest in an investment.

2. Expropriation may be either direct or indirect:
  (a) Direct expropriation occurs when a State takes an investor's property outright, including by nationalisation, compulsion of law or seizure;
  (b) Indirect expropriation occurs when a State takes an investor's property in a manner equivalent to direct expropriation, in that it deprives the investor in substance of the use of the investor's property, although the means used fall short of those specified in subparagraph (a) above.

3. **In order to constitute indirect expropriation, the State's deprivation of the investor's property must be:**
  (a) **Either severe or for an indefinite period; and**
  (b) **Disproportionate to the public purpose.**

4. **A deprivation of property shall be particularly likely to constitute indirect expropriation where it is either:**
  (a) **Discriminatory in its effect, either as against the particular investor or against a class of which the investor forms part; or**
  (b) **In breach of the State's prior binding written commitment to the investor, whether by contract, licence, or other legal document.**

5. Except in rare circumstances to which paragraph 4 applies, such measures taken in the exercise of a State's regulatory powers as may be reasonably justified in the protection of the public welfare, including public health, safety and the environment, shall not constitute an indirect expropriation." (Emphasis added.)

The relevant provisions typically:

(a) Define the concepts of direct and indirect expropriation;

(b) Clarify that expropriation occurs with respect to tangible or intangible property rights and property rights in an investment, which is a somewhat narrower notion than the term investments;

(c) Clarify that an assessment of indirect expropriation involves a case-by-case factual inquiry which involves a balancing of factors, such as:

    (i)   Economic impact of the measure;

    (ii)   Interference with distinct and reasonable investment-backed expectations; and

    (iii)   Nature and characteristics of the measure;

(d) Establish a presumption of the non-expropriatory nature with respect to non-discriminatory measures of general application designed and applied to protect public welfare objectives.

Additional elements or concepts used in some IIAs as criteria to distinguish between indirect expropriation and non-compensable regulation are the notions of proportionality and breach of previous commitments to the investor. Importantly, even if a particular treaty does not contain special provisions on indirect expropriation, tribunals may draw upon the criteria identified above as an expression of the views of a growing number of States.

This section will first look at the three main elements to assess an indirect expropriation, including the relevant arbitral practice:

(a) The economic impact of the measure;

    (b) The extent to which the measure interferes with distinct, reasonable investment-backed expectations;

    (c) The nature, purpose and character of the measure.

1. Factor 1: impact of the measure

To be considered expropriatory, a measure or a series of measures must have a destructive and long-lasting effect on the economic value of the investment and its benefit to the investor. The arbitral tribunal in *Telenor v. Hungary* pointed out that the determinative factors for establishing an expropriation were the intensity and duration of the economic deprivation suffered by the investor.[1]

It is a debated issue whether an effective deprivation alone automatically constitutes an expropriation (the "sole effects" doctrine, for details see section II.A.1(iv)). The clear trend in IIAs is to explicitly state the contrary: the mere fact that a measure or a series of measures have an adverse effect on the economic value of the investment does not necessarily imply that an indirect expropriation has occurred (see treaty examples in box 6). An effective deprivation is a necessary and an important condition, but not a sufficient one.

As discussed above, an indirect expropriation must be equivalent in its effects to a direct expropriation. The impact of the measure or degree of interference must be such as to render the property rights useless, i.e. to deprive the owner of the benefit and economic use of the investment. Arbitral tribunals have overwhelmingly accepted this general notion. For example, the tribunal in *CME v. Czech Republic* stated that a deprivation occurs whenever a State takes steps *"that effectively neutralize the benefit of the property for the foreign owner"*.[2]

Various formulations that have been used to describe the required type of deprivation – an interference that *"deprives the owner of fundamental rights of ownership"*; *"makes rights practically useless"*; *"is sufficiently restrictive to warrant a conclusion that the property has been taken"*; *"deprives, in whole or in significant part, the use or reasonably-to-be-expected economic benefit of the property"*; *"radically deprives the economical use and enjoyment of an investment, as if the rights related thereto had ceased to exist"*; *"makes any form of exploitation of the property disappear"* and *"the property can no longer be put to reasonable use"* (Fortier and Drymer 2004, p. 305). The sense conveyed by these various formulations is that interference must be equal to or approach total impairment and not simply be significant or substantial, as some tribunals have suggested. In other words, *"the affected property must be impaired to such an extent that it must be seen as 'taken'"*.[3]

In the majority of cases to date, claims of indirect expropriation have been dismissed because the negative impact of the measure did not rise to the level of a taking. It has been noted that *"although regulatory measures designed to protect the environment, health and safety or ensure fair competition frequently impose regulatory and compliance costs on an investment, these will not normally reach the threshold of a substantial deprivation"*. (Newcombe and Paradell, 2009, p. 357).

For the correct analysis of a claim, it is important to identify correctly the object of expropriation, i.e. the investment in respect of which the expropriation is alleged (see also section I.E). For instance, in the *Waste Management v. Mexico* case, which involved breaches of contractual obligations by the Mexican city of Acapulco, the tribunal analysed whether these breaches resulted in the expropriation of the claimant's enterprise (investment). It agreed with the claimant that *"the City's breaches ... had the effect of depriving Acaverde [the claimant's enterprise] of 'the reasonably-*

to-be-expected economic benefit' of the project".[4] However, it declined to find that an expropriation of the enterprise had occurred, given that there was no expropriation of the enterprise's physical assets which had been "*sold off in apparently orderly way*" and that the enterprise had never been seized or its activity blocked.[5] The tribunal concluded that "*the loss of benefits or expectations [under a contract] is not a sufficient criterion for an expropriation [of an enterprise]*".[6]

In considering whether a deprivation has occurred, the following questions need to be answered:

(a) Has the measure resulted in a total or near-total destruction of the investment's economic value?
(b) Has the investor been deprived of the control over the investment? and
(c) Are the effects of the measure permanent? The following sections consider these three questions in turn, followed by a separate discussion of the sole effects doctrine.

1.1 Decrease in value

Destruction of the economic value of the investment must be total or close to total. In *Pope & Talbot v. Canada*, the test used by the arbitral tribunal to establish indirect expropriation was "*whether the interference is sufficiently restrictive to support a conclusion that the property has been taken from the owner*".[7] This approach has been followed in other cases. In *Vivendi v. Argentina II*, the tribunal observed that the "*weight of authority ... appears to draw a distinction between only a partial deprivation of value (not an expropriation) and a complete or near complete deprivation of value (expropriation)*".[8] The *LG&E v. Argentina* tribunal recalled that "*in many arbitral decisions, compensation has been denied when it [the State's measure] has not affected all or almost all the investment's economic value*".[9] In *Sempra v. Argentina*, the tribunal explained that the value of the business had to be *"virtually annihilated"*.[10] In *CMS v. Argentina*, the tribunal opined that the relevant test was *"whether the enjoyment of the property has been effectively neutralized"*.[11]

In *Glamis Gold v. United States,* the claimant alleged that the United States, through federal and State measures designed to protect Native American lands, expropriated its rights to mine for gold in south-eastern California. Given that the claimant remained formally in possession of its rights and title, the critical point for the tribunal was to determine whether the mining rights had lost economic value. The tribunal concluded that after the alleged expropriatory measures the project retained a value in excess of $20 million (claimant submitted that the project had had a value of $49.1 million immediately prior to the alleged expropriation). The tribunal thus dismissed the expropriation claim, having concluded that *"the first factor in any expropriation analysis is not met: The complained measures did not cause a sufficient economic impact to the Imperial Project to effect an expropriation of the Claimant's investment"*.[12] Similarly, in *Total v. Argentina*, the tribunal rejected the expropriation claim on the ground that the claimant *"has not shown that the negative economic ... impact of the Measures has been such as to deprive its investment of all or substantially all its value"*.[13]

The income-producing nature of investments may pose a challenging problem when a State measure extinguishes the ability to generate profits but leaves an investor's physical assets intact. The question is whether the loss of income can be viewed as a separate investment or whether the impact should be assessed by reference to the overall investment that includes physical assets. As a general matter, it would seem that the future income is not an asset capable of separate economic exploitation (see section I.E.2) and the assessment of the impact that the measure has on the value of investment must take into account the residual value of physical assets as well as other expenditures made as part of the investment.[14] This would mean that the requisite level of near-total deprivation would need to be reached with respect to the investment as a whole.

1.2   Loss of control over the investment

It has been held that an expropriation claim may be accepted not because of a decrease in value of investment, but because of a loss of control, which prevents the investor from using or disposing of its investment. An investor may lose control of the investment by losing rights of ownership or management, even if the legal title is not affected.

Loss of control is thus a factor that is alternative to destruction of value. It is particularly relevant in situations where the investment is a company or a shareholding in a company. The tribunal noted in *Sempra v. Argentina* that "*a finding of indirect expropriation would require ... that the investor no longer be in control of its business operation, or that the value of the business has been virtually annihilated*".[15] A valuable investment would be useless to the owner if he cannot use, enjoy or dispose of such an investment.

In the practice of the Iran-United States Claims Tribunal, there were a number of cases where the usurpation of management by a State, or the substitution by a State of the foreign investor's management with its own, were analysed as an expropriation. In *Sedco v. National Iranian Oil Co.*,[16] the Tribunal found that an expropriation of the claimant's investment occurred when Iran appointed temporary directors to control and manage the claimant's company and prevented the claimant from accessing the company's funds or participating in its control or management. In *ITT Industries v. Iran*[17] and *Starrett Housing*[18] the Tribunal held that the assumption of control over the claimant's assets by government-appointed managers, which rendered the claimant's rights of ownership meaningless, amounted to an effective expropriation.

Expulsion from the host State of an enterprise's key officers may also be seen as an expropriatory act that leads to the loss of control over the investment. In *Biloune v. Ghana*,[19] the expulsion of Mr. Biloune, who played a critical role in promoting, financing and managing a company engaged in a restaurant/resort project, effectively prevented the company from pursuing the project. The tribunal viewed this act as the culmination of a creeping expropriation.

The tribunal in *Pope & Talbot v. Canada* compiled a list of examples of undue interference with the control over a business: interference with the day-to-day operations of the investment, detention of employees or officers of the investment or supervision of their work, taking of the proceeds of company sales, interference with management or shareholders' activities, preventing a company from paying dividends to its shareholders and interference with the appointment of directors or management of the company.[20] This list simply provides some indications, and it would need to be established in each case whether the relevant State conduct has resulted in the loss of control over the investment.

Several claims have been rejected on the grounds that the clamant retained control over its investment. For instance, in *Feldman v. Mexico*, an exporter of cigarettes from Mexico was allegedly denied tax refund benefits. The tribunal found that there was no expropriation (although it found a breach of the national treatment provision) since *"the regulatory action has not deprived the claimant of control of his company, interfered directly in the internal operations of the company or displaced the Claimant as the controlling shareholder"*.[21] In *CMS v. Argentina*, the investment (shareholding in a gas transportation company) suffered from a significant decrease in value, but the tribunal dismissed the expropriation claim in light of the fact that the investor retained full ownership and control of the shareholding. [22] In *Methanex v. USA*,[23] the tribunal found that there was no expropriation because the investor retained control of its subsidiaries and remained able to sell gasoline additive outside the state of California. Tribunals in *Azurix v. Argentina*,[24] *LG&E v. Argentina*[25] and *AES v. Hungary*[26] rejected expropriation claims on similar grounds.

1.3 Duration of the measure

In order to constitute an expropriation, the measure should be definitive and permanent. A measure that leads to a temporary diminution in value or loss of control would normally not be viewed as expropriatory. As noted by the *Tecmed v. Mexico* tribunal, "*it is understood that the measures adopted by a State, whether regulatory or not, are an indirect de facto expropriation if they are irreversible and permanent ...*".[27]

In *SD Myers v. Canada*, the investor claimed that a ban on the export of a chemical substance (polychlorinated biphenyls, PCB) from Canadian territory constituted an indirect expropriation, as the claimant's business (PCB disposal in the United States) rested precisely on such exports. Although the tribunal found a breach of the national treatment and fair and equitable treatment provisions, it dismissed the expropriation claim because the measure was temporary in its effect:

> "*In this case, the Interim Order and the Final Order were designed to, and did, curb SDMI's initiative, **but only for a time**. ... An opportunity was delayed. The Tribunal concludes that this is not an expropriation case.*"[28] (Emphasis added.)

Equally, in *Suez v. Argentina*, the tribunal found that the measures taken by Argentina to cope with the financial crisis "*did not constitute a permanent and substantial deprivation*" of the investments.[29]

However, some of the de jure temporary measures may also be considered expropriatory depending on the specific circumstances of the case. As noted in the explanatory note to Article 10(3) of the Harvard Draft Convention on the International Responsibility of States for Injuries to Aliens (1961), whether an interference might amount to indirect expropriation will depend on its extent and duration, but "*there obviously comes a stage at which an objective observer would conclude that there is no immediate prospect that the owner will be able to resume the enjoyment of his property*". It was on these grounds that the Iran-United States Claims Tribunals found in a number of cases that the appointment of "temporary" managers constituted a taking, particularly because the surrounding circumstances after the Islamic revolution gave no realistic prospect that the investors could resume their business activity.

1.4   Explicitly rejecting the "sole effects" doctrine

According to an approach taken by some tribunals and known as the "sole effects" doctrine, the effect of the governmental action on the investment is the only factor to be considered when determining whether an indirect expropriation has occurred. The motivation behind the measures is irrelevant.

The *Nykomb Synergetics v. Latvia* tribunal described this approach as follows:

> "*The Tribunal finds that 'regulatory takings' may under the circumstances amount to expropriation or the equivalent of an expropriation. **The decisive factor for drawing the border line towards expropriation must primarily be the degree of possession taking or control over the enterprise the disputed measures entail.***"[30] (Emphasis added.)

The tribunal in *Fireman's Fund v. Mexico*, when summarizing its understanding of current law of expropriation under

NAFTA, stated that *"[t]he effects of the host State's measures are dispositive, not the underlying intent, for determining whether there is expropriation"*.[31]

While it is not clear whether these tribunals actually endorsed a plain "sole effects" doctrine, they did emphasize the importance of the decisive role of the impact of the measure on the investment.

In a move preventing the spread of the "sole effects" approach, the Canada and United States model BITs of 2004 were the first ones to include a provision that explicitly rejected this doctrine with respect to indirect expropriations. Other countries have followed suit by adopting an identical or very similar language in their recent IIAs (see examples in box 8).

Indeed, while the severity of the impact and the degree of interference will be a central factor in determining whether a measure is tantamount to a taking, it is not the decisive or exclusive one. As discussed in section II.A.3, the nature and character of the measure are equally important.

The *SD Myers v. Canada* tribunal noted that *"[t]he general body of precedent usually does not treat regulatory action as amounting to expropriation"* and added that a finding of expropriation requires a look *"at the real interests involved and the purpose and effect of the government measure"*.[32] More recently, in *LG&E v. Argentina*, the tribunal held as follows:

> *"The question remains as to whether one should only take into account the effects produced by the measure **or if one should consider also the context within which a measure was adopted and the host State's purpose.** It is this Tribunal's opinion that there must be a balance in the analysis both of the causes and the effects of a measure in*

order that one may qualify a measure as being of an expropriatory nature."[33] (Emphasis added.)

Box 8. Rejection of the "sole effects" doctrine

Colombia-India BIT (2009)

Article 6
"[...]
b. The determination of whether a measure or series of measures of a Contracting Party constitute indirect expropriation requires a case-by-case, fact-based inquiry considering:

*(i) the economic impact of the measure or series of measures; however, **the sole fact of a measure or series of measures having adverse effects on the economic value of an investment does not imply that an indirect expropriation has occurred**; [...]"* (Emphasis added.)

ASEAN Comprehensive Investment Agreement (2009)
Annex 2

"[...]
3. The determination of whether an action or series of actions by a Members State, in a specific fact situation, constitutes an expropriation ... requires a case-by-case, fact-based inquiry that considers, among other factors:

*a) the economic impact of the government action, **although the fact that an action or series of actions by a Member State has an adverse effect on the economic value of an investment, standing alone, does not establish that such an expropriation has occurred**; [...]"* (Emphasis added.)

There are State acts which – even if they reach the level of total deprivation – do not constitute expropriation under international law and are therefore non-compensable. International law draws a line, albeit not a clear and precise one, between expropriations on the one hand, and legitimate non-compensable measures on the other. This issue is further discussed in section II.B.

2.   Factor 2: interference with investor's expectations

Another relevant factor used in IIAs to guide the determination of whether a measure or series of measures amounts to an indirect expropriation relates to the existence of expectations on the part of the investor that a certain type of act or measure will not be taken by the host State. It requires an evaluation of whether the measure interferes with an investor's reasonable investment-backed expectations, particularly where they are created by assurances given by the State.

In IIA arbitrations, the notion of legitimate expectations has gained particular prominence in the context of the fair and equitable treatment standard (see UNCTAD, 2012). However, this concept has a role to play when considering expropriation claims too – both on the national and international level. Recent research, which focused on a number of national jurisdictions and on experiences of the European Court of Human Rights and the EU, has concluded that *"one important factor for the court's assessment [of an expropriation claim] is whether the individual has some form of legitimate expectation that his or her rights will not be regulated or restricted in a certain way"* (Perkams, 2010, p. 149). A number of recent investment treaties mention legitimate expectations as a factor that must be considered when deciding a claim of indirect expropriation (box 9).

Box 9. References to investor's expectations

China-Colombia BIT (2008)

Article 4
"[...]
b) The determination of whether a measure or series of measures of a Contracting Party constitute indirect expropriation requires a case-by-case, fact-based inquiry considering:
[...]
*ii) The scope of the measure or series of measures **and their interference on the reasonable and distinguishable expectations concerning the investment;*** [...]*" (Emphasis added.)

ASEAN Comprehensive Investment Agreement (2009)
Annex 2

"[...]
3. The determination of whether an action or series of actions by a Members State, in a specific fact situation, constitutes an expropriation ... requires a case-by-case, fact-based inquiry that considers, among other factors:
[...]
*(b) Whether the government action breaches the government's **prior binding written commitment to the investor** whether by contract, license or other legal document*; [...]*" (Emphasis added.)

Australia-Chile FTA (2008)
Annex 10-B: Expropriation
"[...]
3(a) The determination of whether an action or series of actions by a Party, in a specific fact situation, constitutes an indirect expropriation, requires a case-by-case, fact-based inquiry that considers, among other factors:
[...]
*(ii) **The extent to which the measure or series of measures interfere with distinct, reasonable, investment-backed expectations;*** [...]*" (Emphasis added.)

A core part of the analysis regarding any alleged legitimate expectations is to identify their basis. For some tribunals, legitimate expectations need not to be based on specific and explicit undertakings or representations of the host State; implicit assurances, coupled with the investor's assumptions would be sufficient under this view.[34] By contrast, other tribunals require *"specific commitments given by the regulating government to the then putative foreign investor contemplating investment that the government would refrain from such regulation"*.[35] (Emphasis added.) The latter approach is to be preferred; implicit assurances in most circumstances would not provide a sufficient basis for legitimate expectations, especially if the assurances are unofficial or unspecific. Generally, for purposes of expropriation claims, investment tribunals have used a high threshold concerning investor expectations (Reinisch, 2008, p. 448). This means that a legitimate expectation may arise primarily from a State's specific representations or commitments made to the investor concerned, on which the latter has relied.[36]

Investors – be they foreign or domestic – remain exposed to the variety of risks in the country they operate, including the risk of changes in the regulatory environment. As the *Waste Management v. Mexico* tribunal put it, *"it is not the function of the international law of expropriation to eliminate the normal commercial risks of a foreign investor"*.[37] (Emphasis added.) Or as noted in the *Continental Casualty v. Argentina* decision, any reliance by a foreign investor that the legislation is not to be changed would be misplaced.[38] When refusing the expropriation claim arising out of a regulatory measure, the *Methanex v. United States* tribunal emphasized that:

> *"Methanex entered a political economy in which it was widely known, if not notorious, that governmental environmental and health protection institutions at the federal and state level ... continuously monitored the use*

and impact of chemical compounds and commonly prohibited or restricted the use of some of those compounds for environmental and/or health reasons."[39]

The degree of risk to which investor continues to be exposed depends on the type of investment, the regulatory context, the characteristics and institutional particularities of the host country and other relevant factors – political, economic and social, as well as the level of development.

Assessment of legitimate expectations is by no means an exclusive test to be applied to an alleged indirect expropriation (Paulsson and Douglas, 2004, p. 157). In particular, legitimate expectations cannot be assessed in isolation from the character of the governmental action or its economic impact (Newcombe, 2005, p. 38).

3.   Factor 3: nature, purpose and character of the measure

The nature, purpose and character of a measure at issue are also relevant elements to be taken into account in considering whether an indirect expropriation has occurred. They are particularly important in distinguishing between an indirect expropriation and a valid regulatory act, which is not subject to compensation.

Many recent treaties have explicitly introduced these criteria (although the wording may differ) in the assessment of State conduct that is challenged as constituting an indirect expropriation (box 10).

Box 10. Nature, objectives and characteristics of the measure

Canada-Romania BIT (2009)

Annex B: Clarification of indirect expropriation
"[…]
*(b) The determination of whether a measure or series of measures of
a Contracting Party constitute an indirect expropriation requires a
case-by-case, fact-based inquiry that considers, among other
factors:*
[…]
*(iii) **The character of the measure or series of measures, including
their purpose and rationale;** […]"* (Emphasis added.)

Colombia-India BIT (2009)

Article 6
"[…]
*The determination of whether a measure or series of measures of a
Contracting Party constitute indirect expropriation requires a case-
by-case, fact-based inquiry considering:*
[…]
***the character and intent of the measures or series of measures,
whether they are for bona fide public interest purposes or not and
whether there is a reasonable nexus between them and the
intention to expropriate.****"* (Emphasis added.)

ASEAN Comprehensive Investment Agreement (2009)

Annex 2
"[…]
*3. The determination of whether an action or series of actions by a
Members State, in a specific fact situation, constitutes an
expropriation … requires a case-by-case, fact-based inquiry that
considers, among other factors:*
[…]
*(c) **The character of the government action, including its objective
and whether the action is disproportionate to the public purpose
referred to in Article 14(1).****"* (Emphasis added.)

The nature of the measure refers to whether it is a bona fide regulatory act. The purpose focuses on whether the measure genuinely pursues a legitimate public-policy objective. The character of a measure includes features such as non-discrimination, due process and proportionality.

In performing this analysis, different questions may need to be answered: What is the intent of the measure? Does it pursue a genuine public purpose? Is there a reasonable nexus between the purpose and the effect of the measure, i.e. is the measure proportionate? Has it been implemented in a non-discriminatory manner and in compliance with due-process principles? In the end, it needs to be decided whether the measure at issue is targeted and irregular or a common and normal exercise of regulatory powers of the State.

Some tribunals have mentioned that the lack of intent to expropriate is not a key factor in determining whether a measure constitutes an indirect expropriation.[40] However, intent forms part of the analysis regarding the nature, purpose and character of the measure. An explicit reference to those elements in a treaty requires arbitral tribunals to pay close attention, inter alia, to the issue of intent.

B.   Asserting the State's right to regulate in the public interest

The task of distinguishing between non-compensable regulation, on the one hand, and indirect expropriation, on the other, is one of the key issues in modern international investment law. It has long been accepted in international law that State acts are in principle not subject to compensation when they are an expression of the police powers of the State. This section first discusses the doctrine of police powers. It then reviews the relevant recent treaty practice and discusses factors that point to the expropriatory character of a prima facie non-compensable measure.

1. The police powers doctrine in its contemporary meaning

According to the doctrine of police powers, certain acts of States are not subject to compensation under the international law of expropriation. Although there is no universally accepted definition, in a narrow sense, this doctrine covers State acts such as (a) forfeiture or a fine to punish or suppress crime; (b) seizure of property by way of taxation; (c) legislation restricting the use of property, including planning, environment, safety, health and the concomitant restrictions to property rights; and (d) defence against external threats, destruction of property of neutrals as a consequence of military operations and the taking of enemy property as part payment of reparation for the consequences of an illegal war (Brownlie, 2008, p. 532; Wortley, 1959, p. 39). For example, if confiscation of property is effected as a sanction for a violation of domestic law by the property owner, this would not be an expropriation. The same would be the case if an establishment is shut down for violations of environmental or health regulations.

In present times, the police powers must be understood as encompassing a State's full regulatory dimension. Modern States go well beyond the fundamental functions of custody, security and protection. They intervene in the economy through regulation in a variety of ways: preventing and prosecuting monopolistic and anticompetitive practices; protecting the rights of consumers; implementing control regimes through licences, concessions, registers, permits and authorizations; protecting the environment and public health; regulating the conduct of corporations; and others. An exercise of police powers by a State may manifest itself in adopting new regulations or enforcing existing regulations in relation to a particular investor.

The regulatory role of States in the modern economy is vital. Indeed,

"[r]etreating as an actor in the management of economic activities, [the State's] role needs to be affirmed as a regulator in order to provide an equitable and stable framework within which markets can develop in a competitive manner. The regulatory authority of governments needs to be safeguarded if the State is to continue to fulfil its essential functions to protect the public interest in areas like the environment, health and safety, market integrity and social policies" (Geiger, 2002, p. 108).

Extensive State practice as well as arbitral awards and academic literature all acknowledge the right of States to engage in regulatory activity, which should not be undermined or restricted by investment treaties. According to the overwhelming majority of doctrinal opinions, the regulatory conduct of States must carry a presumption of validity. The following excerpts are illustrative:

- *"The persistence of the regulatory powers of the host State … is an essential element of the permanent sovereignty of each State over its economy...**Nothing in the language of bilateral investment treaties purports to undermine the permanent sovereignty of States over their economies.**"* (Lowe, 2004, p. 4, emphasis added.)

- *"**State measures, prima facie a lawful exercise of powers of governments, may affect foreign interests considerably without amounting to expropriation.** Thus foreign assets and their use may be subjected to taxation, trade restrictions involving licences and quotas, or measures of devaluation. While special facts may alter cases, in principle such measures are not unlawful and do not constitute expropriation."* (Brownlie, 2008, p. 532; emphasis added.)

- *"It has always been recognized that ordinary measures of taxation, or the imposition of criminal penalties or export controls do not constitute taking that is compensable. Legislation creating regulatory regimes in areas such as antitrust, consumer protection, securities, environmental protection, planning and land use are more common in developed States. **It is well recognised that interference on the basis of such legislation does not constitute compensable taking in situations in which public harm has already resulted or is anticipated**...These regulatory takings are regarded as essential to the efficient functioning of the State... **Regulatory functions are a matter of sovereign right of the host State and there could be no right in international law to compensation or diplomatic protection in respect of such interference.**"* (Sornarajah, 2004, p. 357; emphasis added.)

- *"**International authorities have regularly concluded that no right to compensate arises for reasonable necessary regulations passed for the protection of public health, safety, morals or welfare**"* (Newcombe, 2005, p. 23; emphasis added.)

- *"...It is serious business to dispute a State's claim to regulation. International law traditionally has granted States broad competence in the definition and management of their economies..."* (Weston, 1976, p. 121).

As regards State practice, numerous international texts and instruments can be referred to.

- In the context of the negotiations on the draft Multilateral Agreement on Investment (MAI), the OECD Ministers issued the following Statement: *"Ministers confirm that the MAI must be consistent with the sovereign responsibility of* *governments to conduct domestic policies. **The MAI would establish mutually beneficial international rules which would not inhibit the normal non-discriminatory exercise of regulatory powers by governments and such exercise of regulatory powers would not amount to expropriation.**"*[41] (Emphasis added.)

- *"...**A State is not responsible for the loss of property or for other economic disadvantages resulting from bona fide taxation, regulation, forfeiture for crime, or other action of the kind that is commonly accepted as within the police power of State,** if it is not discriminatory, and is not designed to cause the alien to abandon the property to the State or sell it at a distress price."* (Restatement (Third) of Foreign Relations of the United States, section 712, Comment (g); emphasis added.)

- *"An uncompensated taking of a property of an alien or a deprivation of the use or enjoyment of property of an alien which results from the execution of tax laws; from a general change in the value of currency; from the action of the competent authorities of the State in the maintenance of public order, health, or morality; or from the valid exercise of belligerent rights or otherwise incidental to the normal operation of the laws of the State shall not be considered wrongful, provided... it is not a clear and discriminatory violation of the law of the State concerned... and it is not an unreasonable departure from the principles of justice recognized by the principal legal systems of the world."* (1961 Harvard Draft Convention on International Responsibility of States for Injuries to Aliens, Article 10(5)).

- *"...the Article on Expropriation and Compensation is intended to incorporate into the MAI existing international*

> *legal norms. The reference... to ... 'measures tantamount to expropriation or nationalisation' ...* ***does not establish a new requirement that Parties pay compensation for losses which an investor or investment may incur through regulation, revenue raising and other normal activity in the public interest undertaken by governments.***" (Interpretative note to Article 5 of the draft MAI "Expropriation and Compensation"; emphasis added.)

- "*...any legislative action or administrative action or omission attributable to the host government which has the effect of depriving the holder of a guarantee of his ownership or control of, or a substantial benefit from, his investment,* ***with the exception of non-discriminatory measures of general application which the governments normally take for the purpose of regulating economic activity in their territories.***" (Convention Establishing the Multilateral Investment Guarantee Agency, Article 11(a)(ii); emphasis added.)

There are numerous examples in current investment treaty practice that explicitly recognize the special case of non-discriminatory regulatory measures taken in the public interest and that, as a general rule, such measures cannot be viewed as constituting an indirect expropriation (see treaty examples in section II.B.2).

Investment tribunals have also made pronouncements regarding the uninhibited power of States to regulate in the public interest. In *Sedco, Inc. v. National Iranian Oil. Co.,* the Iran-United States Claims Tribunal referred to "*an accepted principle of international law that a State is not liable for economic injury which is a consequence of bona fide 'regulation' within the accepted police power of States*".[42] (In the case, however, a law authorizing the nationalization of companies whose debts to banks exceeded their net assets was deemed to fall outside of the police powers exception.)

In *Feldman v. Mexico*, the tribunal noted that *"governments must be free to act in the broader public interest through protection of the environment, new or modified tax regimes, the granting or withdrawal of government subsidies, reductions or increases in tariff levels, imposition of zoning restrictions and the like"*, adding that *"reasonable governmental regulation of this type cannot be achieved if any business that is adversely affected may seek compensation, and it is safe to say that customary international law recognizes this"*.[43]

The regulatory capacity of the State was further reaffirmed in *Methanex v. USA*, where a California ban on a gasoline additive (MTBE) was deemed to be a lawful non-compensable regulation. The tribunal stated that:

> *"...as a matter of general international law, a non-discriminatory regulation for a public purpose, which is enacted in accordance with due process and which affects, inter alias, a foreign investor or investment is not deemed expropriatory and compensable unless specific commitments had been given by the regulating government to the then putative foreign investor contemplating investment that the government would refrain from such regulation..."*.[44]

Similarly, in *Saluka v. Czech Republic* the tribunal referred to both the police and regulatory powers of a State:

> *"It is now established in international law that States are not liable to pay compensation to a foreign investor when, in the normal exercise of their regulatory powers, they adopt in a non-discriminatory manner bona fide regulations that are aimed at the general welfare"*.[45]

"The principle that a State does not commit an expropriation and is thus not liable to pay compensation to a dispossessed alien investor when it adopts general regulations that are 'commonly accepted as within the police power of States' forms part of customary international law today."[46]

In *Suez v. Argentina*, the tribunal also acknowledged that:

"...States have a legitimate right to exercise their police powers to protect the public interest and that the doctrine of police powers ... has been particularly pertinent in cases of expropriation where tribunals have had to balance an investor's property rights with the legitimate and reasonable need for the State to regulate."[47]

In *Chemtura v. Canada*, a manufacturer of a lindane-based pesticide challenged the ban on lindane introduced by Canada. The tribunal found – in addition to the fact that the measures did not amount to a substantial deprivation of the claimant's investment – that:

*"[The relevant State agency] took measures within its mandate, in a non-discriminatory manner, motivated by the increasing awareness of the dangers presented by lindane for human health and the environment. A measure adopted under such circumstances is a **valid exercise of the State's police powers and, as a result, does not constitute an expropriation"*.[48] (Emphasis added.)

In sum, the support for the police powers doctrine appears to be overwhelming. Expropriation provisions in IIAs may not be read as preventing States from bona fide regulation in the public interest. Indeed, many recent IIAs explicitly recognize that they also set forth certain conditions for a measure to be considered non-expropriatory. However, the absence of explicit language to that end does not change the underlying principle, which is strongly enshrined in customary international law. Relevant treaty practice is reviewed in the following section.

2.   Treaty practice: distinguishing non-compensable regulatory measures from indirect expropriations

As discussed above, the nature, purpose and character of a measure play a decisive role in distinguishing between an indirect expropriation and a regulatory act that is not subject to compensation. Recent treaty practice demonstrates attempts to single out bona fide public-interest measures in order to prevent their challenges by investors. Two main treaty approaches may be distinguished in this regard.

A number of treaties have taken the approach of adding a relevant explanatory clause (in an annex or in the expropriation provision itself). It is often phrased as follows:

"Except in rare circumstance, non discriminatory regulatory actions by a Party that are designed and applied to protect legitimate public welfare objectives, such as public health, safety, and the environment, do not constitute indirect expropriations."

Such wording is found in the annexes of many IIAs concluded by Canada and the United States, e.g. Canada-Jordan BIT (2009), Canada-Peru BIT (2006), Canada-Slovak Republic BIT (2010), Australia-United States FTA (2004), CAFTA-DR FTA (2004), Chile-United States FTA (2003), Morocco-United States FTA (2004), Rwanda-United States BIT (2008) and others.

Recent treaties concluded by other countries also include similar language. For instance, Belgium/Luxembourg-Colombia BIT (2009) provides in Article IX(3)(c):

"Except in rare circumstances, such as when a measure or series of measures are so severe in the light of their purpose that they cannot be reasonably viewed as having been adopted and applied in good faith, non-discriminatory measures of a Party that are designed and applied for public purposes or with objectives such as public health, safety and environment protection, do not constitute indirect expropriation".

This formulation requires, inter alia, an assessment of the severity of the measure and its bona fide nature.

Relevant clauses usually describe those measures that do not constitute an indirect expropriation and, therefore, are non-compensable. Some clauses additionally set out conditions or criteria that would render a measure expropriatory that is prima facie non-compensable. The Protocol to the India-Latvia BIT (2010) provides:

*"(b) Actions by a Government or Government controlled bodies, taken as a part of normal business activities, will not constitute indirect expropriation **unless it is prima facie apparent that it was taken with an intent to create an adverse impact on the economic value of an investment**."* (Emphasis added.)

Article 6.2(c) of the BIT between Colombia and the United Kingdom (2010) pursues the same objective but adopts a different formulation:

"Non-discriminatory measures that the Contracting Parties take for reasons of public purpose or social interest (which shall have a meaning compatible with that of 'public purpose') including for reasons of public health, safety, and environmental protection, which are taken in good faith, which are not arbitrary and which are not disproportionate

in light of their purpose, shall not constitute indirect expropriation".

This language is characterized by a number of conditions that a measure has to comply with, including non-discrimination, good faith, non-arbitrariness and proportionality.

It should be noted that such clarification clauses do not constitute an exception to the treaty or to the expropriation provision. They are meant to serve merely as guidance in the assessment of whether a measure constitutes indirect expropriation.

Importantly, even though the relevant clarifications are legally confined to those treaties where they are made, the exemption of good faith non-discriminatory regulatory measures exists in general customary international law on the basis on the police powers doctrine (see section II.B.1). Indeed, many treaties specify that the clarifications with respect to indirect expropriations are "*intended to reflect customary international law concerning the obligation of States with respect to expropriation*" (see United States model BIT, annex B, and provisions in other treaties modelled on it). Criteria for the delineation of such measures formulated by investment tribunals are similar to the ones that can be found in recent treaties. In *Fireman's Fund v. Mexico*, the tribunal – summarizing the law of expropriation under NAFTA (which does not have additional clarificatory language on regulatory measures) – stated as follows:

> "*To distinguish between a compensable expropriation and a non-compensable regulation by a host State, the following factors (usually in combination) may be taken into account: whether the measure is within the recognized police powers of the host State; the (public) purpose and effect of the measure; whether the measure is discriminatory; the proportionality between the means employed and the aim*

sought to be realized; and the bona fide nature of the measure."[49]

The second treaty approach has been to introduce so-called general exceptions, which exclude from the scope of the treaty as a whole government measures necessary for, or relating to, certain public policy objectives. Such general exceptions clauses are often modelled on Article XX of the General Agreement on Tariffs and Trade (GATT) and Article XIV of the General Agreement on Trade in Services (GATS). They often include objectives such as the protection of human or animal or plant life or health, the conservation of exhaustible natural resources and the protection of public morals. Relevant examples can be found in the India-Republic of Korea Comprehensive Economic Partnership Agreement (CEPA) (2009, Article 10.18(1)); India-Singapore Comprehensive Economic Cooperation Agreement (2005, Article 6.11); Canada-Jordan BIT (2009, Article 10(1); ASEAN-China Investment Agreement (2009, Article 16(1); Malaysia-Pakistan Comprehensive Economic Partnership (2007, Article 99); Peru-Singapore FTA (2008, Article 18.1(2)); Panama- Taiwan Province of China FTA (2003, Article 20.02(2)); Malaysia-New Zealand FTA (2009, Article 17.1(1); Japan-Switzerland EPA (2009, Article 95) (see box 11).

If a tribunal establishes that the challenged measure falls within one of the exceptions, it appears that the State may not be held liable for violating any of the treaty's other provisions (substantive protections).[50]

General exceptions usually come with safety valves which ensure that the exceptions are not abused by the State. For instance, the Canada model BIT provides in the chapeau of Article 10 that the measures concerned must not be applied "*in a manner that would constitute arbitrary or unjustifiable discrimination between investments or between investors, or a disguised restriction on international trade or investment*". Other IIAs that incorporate general exceptions include similar provisos.

While being a progressive and balanced solution, the limitation of this approach is that it carves out only measures that relate to public policy objectives specifically mentioned in the general exceptions clause. Potentially, there might be public-interest measures that do not fall within the scope of the listed exceptions but which still must be considered non-expropriatory and non-compensable. Therefore, some countries, such as Canada and India, have combined the two approaches – a clarification clause with respect to indirect expropriation and a general exceptions provision.

Box 11. General exceptions

India-Republic of Korea CEPA (2009)

Article 10.18: Exceptions

"1. Subject to the requirement that such measures are not applied in a manner which would constitute a means of arbitrary or unjustifiable discrimination between States where like conditions prevail, or a disguised restriction on investors and investments, nothing in this Chapter shall be construed to prevent the adoption or enforcement by any Party of measures:

(a) Necessary to protect public morals or to maintain public order;

(b) Necessary to protect human, animal or plant life or health, or the environment;

(c) Necessary to secure compliance with laws and regulations which are not inconsistent with the provisions of this Chapter;

(d) Necessary to protect national treasures of artistic, historic or archaeological value; or

(e) Necessary to conserve exhaustible, natural resources if such measures are made effective in conjunction with restrictions on domestic production or consumption."

---

3.   Presumption of validity of a regulatory measure

The critical issue, as the *Saluka v. Czech Republic* tribunal put it, lies in identifying *"in a comprehensive and definite fashion precisely what regulations are considered permissible and commonly accepted as falling within the police power or regulatory power of States and thus, non-compensable"*.[51] The challenge is old but still unsettled. Even though international law does not offer a conclusive answer, a general conceptual framework can be advanced based on the elements that have emerged.

It should be noted from the outset that a valid regulatory act is not an exception to international liability. It must be seen as a measure that simply does not trigger international liability.

To assess a particular measure (be it a new regulation or application of an existing one to a specific investor), it is necessary to undertake a broad examination of its nature, purpose and character. The critical issue is to determine whether the measure is part of the normal or common regulatory activity of the State or whether it possesses attributes that turn it into an expropriation.

An act of general application and its individual application enjoys a presumption of validity. Under international law, States are presumed to act in good faith unless shown otherwise. As one commentator put it:

> "*It is serious business to dispute a State's claim to regulation. International law traditionally has granted States broad competence in the definition and management of their economies, and no State, therefore, is likely to take lightly a challenge to what it contends is liability-free behaviour. The venerable innocent-before-proven-guilty presumption is not one that shapes action and reaction only among individuals in the criminal law sphere. It has its equivalents, and rightly so, on the international plane.*"
> (Weston, 1976, p. 121.)

The exercise of the police or regulatory power may be the subject of a legitimate complaint and an international tribunal should be able to make an independent determination, but "*if the reasons given are valid and bear some plausible relationship to the action taken, no attempt may be made to search deeper to see whether the State was activated by some illicit motive*" (Christie, 1962, p. 338).

In some circumstances, a regulation may constitute a disguised form of a taking. States should not escape responsibility by simply characterizing a measure as a regulation. A way of assessing whether a particular measure departs from the normal activity of the State is to examine it against the indicators that point to its expropriatory nature. Given the presumption of validity, the burden is on the investor to demonstrate that the measure is in fact mala fide, fails to pursue a genuine public purpose, is discriminatory, violates the due-process requirement or is otherwise irregular. Before the burden of proof shifts to the investor, the State must make a prima facie case to show that a measure pursues a public purpose, is non-discriminatory and was implemented in accordance with due process, and thus that it should be non-compensable, despite the destructive impact on the investment. This is reasonable, given that the State should have at its disposal full information about the measure (Newcombe, 2009, p. 366).

Compliance of the measure with domestic law may not necessarily establish the outcome, as "*an act of State must be characterized as internationally wrongful if it constitutes a breach of an international obligation, even if the act does not contravene the State's internal law*". However, compliance with domestic law may provide additional evidence of validity. As the law of expropriation has essentially grown out of, and mirrored, parallel domestic laws, "*it appears plausible that measures that are, under the rules of the main domestic laws, normally considered regulatory without amounting to expropriation, will not require compensation under international law*" (Dolzer and Schreuer, 2008, p. 95).

Some international instruments suggest, albeit in a very general manner, that the liability of a State arises when it misuses or abuses its authority. For instance, the OECD Draft Convention on the Protection of Foreign Property (1967) states that a taking occurs not as a result of the normal and lawful regulatory conduct, but rather as a result of the misuse of otherwise lawful regulation which deprives an owner of the substance of his rights (Article 3). To a similar effect, the Harvard Draft Convention on the International Responsibility of States for Injury to Aliens (1961) refers, inter alia, to an *"unreasonable departure from the principles of justice"* and *"abuse of powers"* (Article 10(5)).

In these cases, tribunals will have to look for additional factors to establish the illegality and irregularity in the measure. The irregularity may be found in the substance of the measure, in the scope of its application and/or in the way it was adopted. It may also be found in the act of application or individualization of a general regulation, e.g. denials, cancellations or revocations of contracts, licences, permits or concessions with regard to a particular foreign investor.

4.   Indicators of the expropriatory nature of a regulatory measure

The list of these indicators that point to the abnormal or irregular nature of a measure is wide. It includes the lack of genuine public purpose, of due process, of proportionality, and of fair and equitable treatment; discrimination, abuse of rights and direct benefit to the State. No one particular indicator should be treated as decisive: a global assessment is necessary in order to see – against the rather high threshold set by international law – whether the State should be held internationally responsible. This is necessarily a very context-specific exercise. As aptly noted by the tribunal in *Saluka v. Czech Republic*:

> *"Faced with the question of **when, how and at what point an otherwise valid regulation becomes, in fact and effect, an unlawful expropriation**, international tribunals must consider the circumstances in which the question arises.*

The context within which an impugned measure is adopted and applied is critical to the determination of its validity."[52] (Emphasis in the original)

Public purpose, non-discrimination and due process also serve as conditions for the legality of an expropriation (see section I.F). However, in that context, they were designed for cases of direct expropriation where the taking itself is self-evident. For cases involving alleged regulatory expropriations, the same requirements serve to distinguish compensable expropriation from non-compensable regulation and have been recognized as such in many investment treaties and arbitral awards.

4.1   Lack of public purpose, discrimination and lack of due process

A non-discriminatory measure of general application that seeks to attain a legitimate welfare objective and enacted in accordance with due process is prima facie non-compensable. These considerations served as a basis for the decision of the tribunal in the *Methanex* case:

"...the California ban was made for a public purpose, was non-discriminatory and was accomplished with due process. ... From the standpoint of international law, the Californian ban was a lawful regulation and not an expropriation".[53] (Emphasis added.)

To a similar effect, the *Saluka* tribunal referred to *"non-discriminatory manner bona fide regulations that are aimed at the general welfare".*[54] Multiple recent treaties refer to these factors as relevant in the assessment of regulatory measures (see section II.B.2).

As far as public purpose is concerned, the relevant questions to ask are whether the stated purpose is genuine and whether the measure concerned is indeed designed to achieve it. Determination of what is in the public interest of a particular State as well as what measures are suitable to achieve the public purpose are matters in which States enjoy considerable latitude. This has been recognized by arbitral tribunals. For example, in *Tecmed v. Mexico*, the tribunal emphasized the *"due deference"* that must be afforded to States in the matter of *"defining the issues that affect its public policy or the interests of society as a whole, as well as the actions that will be implemented to protect such values".*[55]

Regarding the discrimination element, the *Methanex* tribunal stated that *"an intentionally discriminatory regulation against a foreign investor fulfils a key requirement for establishing expropriation".*[56] The non-discrimination requirement implies the diffusiveness of the impact on different actors and constituencies and serves to prevent singling out or targeting a foreign investor. It primarily concerns nationality-based differentiation but it also seems to cover racial, religious, ethnic and other types of discrimination prohibited under customary international law. It appears that a non-discriminatory regulation which is enforced in a discriminatory manner will also fit the description. Where a formally non-discriminatory regulation is designed in a way that it only covers certain foreign investor or investors, other indicators need to be examined to decide whether the measure is bona fide.

The due process requirement – when applied to regulatory measures of general application – is meant to ensure that the measure is not adopted with serious procedural violations, i.e. that it was passed by a competent State body, supported by the requisite number of votes (e.g. if a parliamentary act is at issue) and so forth. Minor procedural irregularities should not affect the non-compensable nature of the measure.

Depending on the context, there might be other indicators of due process. For example, in *Methanex v. USA*, California's decision to ban MTBE (a gasoline additive) was primarily based on a research report by the University or California, which concluded the use of MTBE presented significant water contamination risks. Relevantly for the question of due process, the tribunal noted that the report was subject to public hearings, testimony and peer review and that its *"emergence as a serious scientific work from such an open and informed debate is the best evidence that it was not the product of a political sham engineered by California"*.[57]

In *EDF v. Romania,* the claimant participated in a joint venture formed with a Romanian entity owned by the Government, engaged in commercial and retails outlet activities at the Otopeni Airport. Following the issuance of new duty-free regulations, the licence of the company was revoked. The company was later declared bankrupt after the Financial Guard imposed a fine and ordered the sequestration of enterprise's assets. The tribunal noted that the confiscation sanction was within the legal power of the Financial Guard and that it was applied in good faith. It took into account that due process had been assured to the claimant by Romania and that the sanction applied by the Financial Guard was due to claimant's failure to comply with procedural requirements.[58]

4.2 Lack of proportionality

The principle of proportionality is not universally recognized as relevant in the expropriation context. At the same time, some recent treaties do refer to the proportionality test (see, for example, the ASEAN Comprehensive Investment Agreement (2009), the Colombia-United Kingdom BIT (2010) and the Colombia-India BIT (2009), all quoted above). Some scholars have called for a greater reliance on the proportionality approach (e.g. Kingsbury and Schill, 2010; Kriebaum, 2007b).

The principle of proportionality is one of the pillars of the European Court of Human Rights when it comes to its practice on the dispossession of property. In the leading case *Sporrong and*

Lönnroth, the Court stated that a *"fair balance"* has to be struck *"between the demands of the general interest of the community and the requirements of the protection of the individual's fundamental rights"*.[59] Accordingly, the Court will inquire into the means chosen to achieve the legitimate aim pursued: *"a measure must be both appropriate for achieving its aim and not disproportionate thereto"*.[60] The requisite balance will be upset when the person concerned has had to bear *"an individual and excessive burden"*[61] or one that is *"disproportionate"*[62] (Ruiz Fabri, 2002, p. 163). The relevant factors of the assessment include *"the severity of the interference, legitimate expectations of the complainant, the suitability of the interference to reach the public purpose, the priority of the public purpose and a special public interest to pay less than full compensation"* (Kriebaum 2007b, p. 730). It must be kept in mind that international law has traditionally afforded States a wide margin of discretion with respect to questions such as priority of the public purpose or suitability of the measure.

In investor-State arbitration, the *Tecmed v. Mexico* case was the first one where the tribunal relied on the proportionality analysis. The dispute arose out of the decision of the environmental authority to deny renewal of a permit to operate a landfill of hazardous waste. After finding that the deprivation had been total, the tribunal proceeded as follows:

> *"...the Arbitral Tribunal will consider, in order to determine if they are to be characterized as expropriatory, whether such actions or measures are proportional to the public interest presumably protected thereby and to the protection legally granted to investments, taking into account that the significance of such impact has a key role upon deciding the proportionality. ... There must be a reasonable relationship of proportionality between the charge or weight imposed to the foreign investor and the*

aim sought to be realized by any expropriatory measure."[63] (Emphasis added.)

For the tribunal, the claimant's breaches on which the State based its denial to renew the permit did not threaten public health or impair the ecological balance. It weighed this fact against the total deprivation of the investment's value and decided that the measure was disproportionate and that, therefore, an indirect expropriation had occurred.

This approach has been followed in some subsequent cases. The *Azurix v. Argentina* tribunal, referring to the practice of the European Court of Human Rights and the *Tecmed* decision, found the proportionality principle to provide *"useful guidance for purposes of determining whether regulatory actions would be expropriatory and give rise to compensation"*.[64] In *LG&E v. Argentina*, the tribunal stated that *"it can generally be said that the State has the right to adopt measures having a social or general welfare purpose. In such a case, **the measure must be accepted without any imposition of liability, except in cases where the State's action is obviously disproportionate to the need being addressed**"*.[65] (Emphasis added.) In these two cases, however, the expropriation claim was dismissed.

It is worth noting that these decisions did not discuss the appropriateness of importing the proportionality test from the human-rights regime to investor-State arbitration. The European Court of Human Rights has a somewhat different logic than investment treaties when it comes to the principle of proportionality using it not only to determine whether or not there has been an expropriation but also to estimate the amount of compensation owed. The use of principles from different regimes may be complimentary and mutually enriching; however, transplantation may be effected only after an assessment of the appropriateness thereof. Importantly, the proportionality analysis implies a far-reaching intrusion into governmental decision-making, including the assessment of such issues as priority of public purpose and suitability of the measure for achieving it. The European Court of Human Rights, as well as national courts would seem to have sufficient legitimacy to undertake a full proportionality analysis. As for ad hoc investor-State tribunals, such legitimacy appears to be lacking, with exception of situations when the applicable IIA specifically instructs them to perform a proportionality assessment or where the proportionality analysis helps to discern a mala fide measure.

4.3   Lack of fair and equitable treatment

When the measure causes total impairment and is found to breach the fair and equitable treatment (FET) provision of the treaty, some tribunals have concluded that the act is expropriatory. In *Vivendi v. Argentina II*, the dispute arouse from a concession agreement that privatized the water and sewage services in the Argentine province of Tucuman. The claimant alleged that an illegitimate campaign, together with a number of provincial measures, made the recovery rate decline dramatically, thus rendering the concession valueless. The tribunal concluded that the claimants had been radically deprived of the economic use and enjoyment of their concessionary rights, namely the right to invoice their customers and pursue payment for the water and sewage services provided under the concession. The determination that the province's measures were unfair and inequitable played a role in the expropriation assessment:

> *"As to this, we find that the Province's unfair and inequitable measures, identified at 7.4 above, which ultimately led to CAA's [Compañia de Aguas del Aconquija S.A., a local affiliate of the investor] notice of rescission of the Concession Agreement on 27 August 1997, struck at the economic heart of, and crippled, Claimants' investment."*[66]

The *Vivendi* case did not concern a regulatory measure; however, this may not change the approach in principle. An FET claim involves an assessment of a given governmental measure against the criteria of due process, interference with legitimate expectations, non-discrimination, arbitrariness and abusiveness towards the investor (UNCTAD, 2012). It is possible that if a regulatory measure is found to be inconsistent with the FET standard, a tribunal will see it as such in the course of the expropriation analysis. However, this approach is questionable. Some tribunals have read the FET standard in an expansive manner and have read additional elements into it (e.g. transparency and consistency); in such cases one may not mechanically import the FET reasoning into the expropriation context.

In practical terms, the qualification of a measure as expropriatory, after it is found to have breached the FET standard, does not alter available remedies. State conduct that is found to be FET-inconsistent becomes internationally unlawful and triggers the obligation of the State to provide reparation. As a general rule, the amount of such reparation will not be different regardless of whether the conduct concerned is held in breach of one or two IIA obligations.

4.4   Abuse of rights (*abus de droit*)

Under the theory of "abuse of rights", the exercise of a right for the sole purpose of causing an injury to another is prohibited. It is a corollary of the principle of good faith which governs the exercise of rights by States (Cheng, 1953, p. 121). Although the principle has been used on several occasions as regards international claims, it is only recently that an investment tribunal relied on it in the expropriation context.

In *Saipem v. Bangladesh*, a dispute arose out of a contract for the construction of a pipeline between Saipem and a public company. The dispute was later settled under an International

Chamber of Commerce (ICC) arbitration in favour of the investor. However, the Supreme Court of Bangladesh declared that the ICC award was *"a nullity on the eye of law"* as it was *"clearly illegal and without jurisdiction"*. The International Centre for Settlement of Disputes (ICSID) tribunal considered that the residual contractual rights contained in the ICC award had been expropriated, as the chances of enforcing the award outside Bangladesh were negligible.

The tribunal concluded that the revocation of the arbitrator's authority was contrary to international law, specifically to the principle of the "abuse of rights" and the New York Convention on the Recognition and Enforcement of Foreign Arbitral Awards, as the Bangladeshi courts had abused their supervisory jurisdiction over the arbitration process. The tribunal held that:

> *"It is generally acknowledged in international law that a State exercising a right for a purpose that is different from that for which that right was created commits an abuse of rights..."*.[67]

The doctrine that precludes State authorities from exercising their rights for an end different from that for which the right has been created, with the result that injury is caused, is also known in some domestic systems as *détournement de pouvoir*. Its essential element lies in the establishment of the motives or intent behind the State's conduct at issue as well as its practical results. In the context of the police powers, if it is established that the true intention is not consistent with the alleged public purpose, the measure can be found to constitute an "abuse of rights". In this sense, the doctrine of "abuse of rights" is a flipside of the requirement that the police-powers measure must pursue a genuine public purpose (see section II.B.4(i)).

4.5   Direct benefit to the State

In some domestic legal systems, the absence or presence of a benefit to the State is a factor that helps determine whether an indirect expropriation has occurred. Thus, whether a constructive acquisition has occurred (whether the measure resulted in a direct benefit to the State) is given significant weight by Canadian courts. In 2006, the Supreme Court of Canada heard a claim concerning the expropriation of land owned by a railway company. Under the facts of the case, the City of Vancouver had adopted a development plan that restricted the use of the land to non-economic uses and effectively froze the development of a parcel of land by the railway company. The company argued that the city's conduct amounted to an effective taking. The Court rejected the claim on the grounds that city had not acquired a beneficial interest relating to the land in question.[68] (It was also noted that the development plan did not remove all reasonable uses of the property.)

In the IIA context, some tribunals have used this factor. For example, in *Olguín v. Paraguay*, the tribunal stated that *"[f]or an expropriation to occur, there must be actions … depriving the affected party of the property it owns, **in such a way that whoever performs those actions will acquire, directly or indirectly, control, or at least the fruits of the expropriated property"***[69] (emphasis added). Other tribunals, by contrast, made statements to the effect that a transfer of assets to the State is not required for an expropriation to be found.[70] This may indeed be so when there are other elements which indicate the irregularity of the measure, like the lack of a genuine public purpose. In other circumstances, the direct-benefit factor may be of relevance. For example, if an economic activity is banned for environmental reasons, this is unlikely to be viewed as a taking; however, if an economic activity is banned for private actors because the government is assuming State monopoly over it, there is direct benefit to the State and, therefore, there would be stronger arguments for a finding of expropriation.

There can be circumstances when the benefit goes not to the expropriating State but to a private person or company that seeks to neutralize a (foreign) competitor. The *Rumeli* tribunal noted, with respect to judicial expropriation, that "*it is usually instigated by a private party for his own benefit, and not that of the State*".[71] In such cases, the State is used as an instrument for private gain (there is no public purpose) and the question of benefit is irrelevant. Finally, when a certain measure benefits the society as a whole, such as general environmental or public-health legislation, there is no appropriation of assets or benefits by an identifiable entity (it is widely dispersed), and thus no expropriation.

C. Steps to assess a claim of indirect expropriation

The analysis undertaken in this paper suggests that a measure allegedly constituting an indirect expropriation can be assessed by going through a sequence of analytical steps.

As a preliminary matter, one needs to establish whether the measure is attributable to the respondent State and if so, whether the latter acted in its sovereign capacity. Secondly, it is important to correctly identify the investment at issue and, in particular, to understand whether it should be considered as part of the investor's overall investment in the host State or whether it is capable of being expropriated separately.

Moving on to the impact of the measure on investment, it needs to be determined whether the State conduct has resulted in a total or near-total deprivation of the investor's investment (loss of investment's value or of investor's control over the investment) and whether the effect of the measure is permanent. An additional factor to be considered here is whether the investor had a legitimate expectation (arising from a written commitment of the host State) that the State would not act the way it did.

If a measure is of a regulatory nature or is an enforcement of existing regulation, one would need to ask the following questions: Does the measure contain the characteristics of a bona fide exercise of police powers by the host State? Is it taken in pursuance of a genuine public purpose, in a non-discriminatory manner and in accordance with the due process of law? Was there a transfer of benefit of the investment of the State or any private party? Is there a manifest disproportionality between the aims pursued and the harm inflicted on the investor?

On the basis of the above-mentioned factors, it should be possible to decide whether an indirect expropriation has taken place or whether the conduct qualifies as the State's non-compensable exercise of police powers and regulatory prerogatives. If expropriation is found, the analysis must proceed to the matters of its lawfulness or unlawfulness and the question of compensation or reparation.

This suggested sequence is not meant as a mechanical tool to be applied in every case regardless of its specific circumstances. Neither is it the only possible approach. Rather, it represents one way of dealing with a claim of indirect expropriation that may prove useful to arbitrators, investors and States alike.

Notes

[1] *Telenor v. Hungary*, Award, 13 September 2006, para. 70.

[2] *CME v. Czech Republic*, Partial Award, 13 September 2001, para. 150.

[3] *GAMI Investments v. Mexico*, Final Award, 15 November 2004, para. 126.

[4] *Waste Management v. Mexico*, Final Award, 30 April 2004, para. 159.

[5] Ibid., paras. 156–157.

[6] Ibid., para. 159. The tribunal then proceeded to examine the question of whether the contract rights themselves were expropriated. It dismissed that claim on different grounds.

[7] *Pope & Talbot v. Canada*, Interim Award, 26 June 2000, para. 102.

[8] *Vivendi v. Argentina II*, Award, 20 August 2007, para. 7.5.11.

[9] *LG&E v. Argentina*, Decision on Liability, 3 October 2006, para. 191.

[10] *Sempra Energy v. Argentina*, Award, 28 September 2007, para. 285.

[11] *CMS v. Argentina*, Award, 12 May 2005, para. 262.

[12] *Glamis Gold, Ltd. v. USA*, Award, 8 June 2009, para. 536.

[13] *Total v. Argentina*, Decision on Liability, 27 December 2010, para. 196.

[14] In *Pope & Talbot v. Canada*, the tribunal found that business income (in that case – based on the ability to sell softwood lumber in the United States market) was an integral part of the value of the enterprise. The tribunal decided that the loss of business income did not result in a "substantial deprivation" of the investor's enterprise as a whole and thus did not constitute an expropriation. (*Pope & Talbot v. Canada*, Interim Award, 26 June 2000, paras. 98 and 102.)

[15] *Sempra Energy v. Argentina*, Award, 28 September 2007, para. 285.

[16] *Sedco, Inc. v. National Iranian Oil Company*, Interlocutory Award, 28 October 1985, 9 the Iran-United States Claims Tribunal Reports 248, p. 278.

[17] *ITT Industries, Inc. v. Iran et al.*, Award, 26 May 1983, 2 Iran-United States Claims Tribunal Reports 348, pp. 351–352.

[18] *Starrett Housing v. Iran*, Interlocutory Award No. ITL 32-24-1, 19 December 1983.

[19] *Biloune v. Ghana*, Award on Jurisdiction and Liability, 27 October 1989.

[20] *Pope & Talbot*, Interim Award, 26 June 2000, para. 100.

[21] *Feldman v. Mexico*, Award on Merits, 16 December 2002, para. 41.

22   *CMS v. Argentina*, Award, 12 May 2005, para. 263.
23   *Methanex v. USA*, Final Award, 3 August 2005.
24   *Azurix v. Argentina*, Award, 14 July 2006.
25   *LG&E v. Argentina*, Decision on Liability, 3 October 2006.
26   *AES v. Hungary*, Award, 23 September 2010, paras. 14.2.1–14.3.4.
27   *Tecmed v. Mexico*, Award, 29 May 2003, para. 116.
28   *SD Myers v. Canada*, First Partial Award, 13 November 2000, paras. 287–288.
29   *Suez et al. v. Argentina*, Decision on Liability, 30 July 2010, para. 129.
30   *Nykomb v. Latvia*, Award, 16 December 2003, para. 4.3.1.
31   *Fireman's Fund v. Mexico*, Award, 17 July 2006, para. 176(f).
32   *S.D. Myers v. Canada*, First Partial Award, 13 November 2000, paras. 281 and 285.
33   *LG&E v. Argentina*, Decision on Liability, 3 October 2006, paras. 189 and 194.
34   *Azurix v. Argentina*, Award, 14 July 2006, paras. 316–322.
35   *Methanex v. USA*, Final Award, 3 August 2005, Part IV, Chapter D, para. 7.
36   The tribunal in *Grand River Enterprises v. USA*, when analysing "legitimate expectations" in the expropriation context, stated that "*[o]rdinarily, reasonable or legitimate expectations of the kind protected by NAFTA are those that arise through targeted representations or assurances made explicitly or implicitly by a State party.*" (Award, 12 January 2011, para. 141, emphasis added.)
37   *Waste Management v. Mexico*, Final Award, 30 April 2004, para. 159.
38   *Continental Casualty v. Argentina*, Award, 5 September 2008, para. 258.
39   *Methanex v. USA*, Final Award, 3 August 2005, Part IV, Chapter D, para. 9.
40   See, for example, *Chemtura Corporation v. Canada*, Award, 2 August 2010, para. 242; *Metalclad v. Mexico*, Award, 30 August 2000, para. 103.
41   Ministerial Statement on the Multilateral Agreement on Investment, 28 April 1998, para. 5.
42   *Sedco, Inc. v. National Iranian Oil Co.*, Interlocutory Award No. ITL 55-129-3, 28 October 1985, 9 the Iran-United States Claims Tribunal Reports 248, p. 275.

43   *Feldman v. Mexico*, Award, 16 December 2002, para. 83.
44   *Methanex Corporation v. the United States*, Final Award, 3 August 2005, part IV, chapter D, para. 7.
45   *Saluka v. the Czech Republic*, Partial Award, 17 March 2006, para. 255.
46   Ibid., para. 262.
47   *Suez et al. v. Argentina*, Decision on Liability, 30 July 2010, para. 147.
48   *Chemtura v. Canada*, Award, 2 August 2010, para. 266.
49   *Fireman's Fund v. Mexico*, Award, 17 July 2006, para. 176(j).
50   Commentators have pointed out that in case of a direct expropriation (for example, for environmental reasons), existence of a general exception presumably does not exclude payment of compensation (Newcombe and Paradell, 2009, p. 506).
51   *Saluka v. Czech Republic*, Partial Award, 17 March 2006, para. 263.
52   *Saluka v. Czech Republic*, Partial Award, 17 March 2006, para. 264.
53   *Methanex v. USA*, Final Award, 3 August 2005, Part IV, Chapter D, paras. 7 and 15.
54   *Saluka v. Czech Republic*, Partial Award, 17 March 2006, para. 255.
55   *Tecmed v. Mexico*, Award, 29 May 2003, para. 122.
56   *Methanex v. USA*, Final Award, 3 August 2005, Part IV, Chapter D, para. 4.
57   *Methanex. v. USA*, Final Award, 3 August 2005, Part IV, Chapter D, para. 101.
58   *EDF v. Romania*, Award, 8 October 2009, para. 313.
59   *Sporrong and Lönnroth v. Sweden*, European Court of Human Rights, Judgment, 23 September 1982, para. 69.
60   *James and Others v. United Kingdom*, European Court of Human Rights, Judgment, 21 February 1986, para. 50.
61   *Sporrong and Lönnroth v. Sweden*, European Court of Human Rights, Judgment, 23 September 1982, para. 73.
62   *Erkner & Hofauer v. Austria*, European Court of Human Rights, Judgment, 23 April 1987, para. 79.
63   *Tecmed v. Mexico*, Award, 29 May 2003, para. 122.
64   *Azurix v. Argentina*, Award, 14 July 2006, para. 312.
65   *LG&E v. Argentina*, Decision on Liability, 3 October 2006, para. 195.
66   *Vivendi v. Argentina II*, Award, 20 August 2007, para. 7.5.25. For another example, see *Metalclad v. Mexico*, Award, 30 August 2000,

para. 104; *Gemplus & Talsud v. Mexico*, Award, 16 June 2010, paras. 8–23.

[67] *Saipem v. Bangladesh*, Award, 30 June 2009, para. 160.

[68] *Canadian Pacific Railway Co. v. Vancouver (City)*, (2006) 1 S.C.R. 227, as discussed in Schwartz and Bueckert, 2006, pp. 489–490.

[69] *Olguín v. Paraguay*, Award, 26 July 2001, para. 84.

[70] See, for example, *Tecmed v. Mexico*, Award, 29 May 2003, para. 113; *Metalclad v. Mexico*, Award, 30 August 2000, para. 103.

[71] *Rumeli v. Kazakhstan*, Award, 29 July 2008, para. 704.

III. REMEDIES AND VALUATION

A. Compensation for lawful expropriation and reparation for unlawful expropriation

As discussed in section I.F, expropriations can be lawful and unlawful. The first is a legitimate act not sanctioned under international law, whereas the second is an international wrongdoing: the first requires compensation, the second, reparation.

As early as 1928, the Permanent Court of International Justice in the *Chorzów* case made a distinction between lawful and unlawful takings and their different financial consequences. It held that, in case of lawful expropriation, the damage suffered must be repaired through the *"payment of fair compensation"* or *"the just price of what was expropriated"* at the time of the expropriation, meaning the *"value of the undertaking at the moment of dispossession, plus interest to the day of payment"*.[1] By contrast, it decided that, *"in case of unlawful expropriation, international law provides for restitutio in integrum or, if impossible, its monetary equivalent at the time of the judgment"*.[2]

The distinction in consequences between lawful and unlawful expropriations was later reaffirmed by the Iran-United States Claims Tribunal in *Amoco v. Iran*[3] and more recently by arbitral tribunals in ISDS cases, including *ADC v. Hungary*,[4] *Siemens v. Argentina*[5] and *Vivendi v. Argentina II*.[6] Under customary international law, lawful takings must be accompanied by "appropriate" compensation, which under some interpretations may justify less than full compensation.[7] Modern investment disputes are brought under investment treaties and the latter set forth an explicit standard of compensation for lawful expropriations (typically "fair market value" or a similar formula) (see section I.F.4 for details).

An unlawful expropriation is, by contrast, a wrongful international act requiring reparation. Investment treaties do not include rules on reparation leaving this matter to customary international law. It is widely accepted that the applicable standard for the assessment of damages resulting from an unlawful act is set out in the decision of the Permanent Court of International Justice in the *Chorzów Factory* case, and later formulated in Article 31 of the Articles on International State Responsibility of the International Law Commission (see box 12).

Box 12. Reparation for international wrongful acts

Chorzów Factory case[8]

"The essential principle contained in the actual notion of an illegal act – a principle which seems to be established by international practice and in particular by the decisions of arbitral tribunals – is that reparation must, as far as possible, wipe out all the consequences of the illegal act and re-establish the situation which would, in all probability, have existed if that act had not been committed. Restitution in kind, or, if this is not possible, payment of a sum corresponding to the value which a restitution in kind would bear; the award, if need be, of damages for loss sustained which would not be covered by restitution in kind or payment in place of it – such are the principles which should serve to determine the amount of compensation due for an act contrary to international law."

International Law Commission, Articles on Responsibility of States for Internationally Wrongful Acts

Article 31. Reparation
"1. The responsible State is under an obligation to make full reparation for the injury caused by the internationally wrongful act. 2. Injury includes any damage, whether material or moral, caused by the internationally wrongful act of a State."

/...

Box 12. (concluded)

Article 34. Forms of reparation
"Full reparation for the injury caused by the internationally wrongful act shall take the form of restitution, compensation and satisfaction, either singly or in combination, in accordance with the provisions of this chapter."

Article 36. Compensation
"1. The State responsible for an internationally wrongful act is under an obligation to compensate for the damage caused thereby, insofar as such damage is not made good by restitution.
2. The compensation shall cover any financially assessable damage including loss of profits insofar as it is established."

The *Chorzów Factory* standard of compensation demands wiping out the consequences of the wrongful act and re-establishing the situation that would have prevailed had the illicit act not occurred. In case of an expropriation, the first remedy is restitution of property, but as it is rarely practical or even feasible, payment of the value of the expropriated investment plus compensation of any consequential losses is the more likely remedy.

The *Chorzów* standard can be difficult to implement in practice because it implies making a speculative assessment.

> *"It requires the comparison between a real situation, on the one hand, and a hypothetical situation, on the other; i.e. how would reality have – in theory – evolved had the unlawful act not occurred. That requires the construction of a hypothetical course of events with necessarily speculative elements."* (Wälde and Sabahi, 2007, p. 6.)

As the arbitral practice shows, reparation can be equal or exceed, but never fall below compensation. Particularly, reparation would be higher than compensation when the loss is greater than the value of the expropriated investment. Although the value of the investment remains the same irrespective of the legality or illegality of the expropriation, reparation may include elements additional to the investment's value in order to "re-establish" the situation following the *Chorzów* standard.

The fact that investment treaties require payment of the fair market value of an investment even in case of a lawful expropriation means that – depending on the valuation method selected (see section III.B) – future profits can well be factored into compensation. This becomes problematic from the policy perspective because the amount of compensation even for a lawful expropriation may become very high and de facto equal to reparation for unlawful expropriation. The practice of the European Court of Human Rights is instructive in this respect – in case of a lawful expropriation, the Court is satisfied with the amount of compensation that is "reasonably related" to the fair market value of the property taken, in other words, not "manifestly below" this value (Ripinsky with Williams, 2008, pp. 81–83). This approach allows States and the Court more discretion in determining a fair amount of compensation for a lawful expropriation, enabling them to take into account specific circumstances of the case and equitable considerations. This is particularly relevant in cases of indirect expropriations which may involve measures at least partially explained by legitimate government considerations and which do not necessarily entail a transfer of economic benefits from an investor to the State.

Under most existing IIAs, if a tribunal finds that an expropriation has occurred, as a matter of law it may not award less than the fair market value of the investment, regardless of the circumstances of the case. The practice whereby a tribunal must grant either full compensation or no compensation at all has been criticized as the all-or-nothing approach where the real balancing of interest is not possible (Kriebaum, 2007b, p. 729). The European Court of Human Rights is more flexible in this regard as it awards less than full compensation in certain situations, e.g. where the expropriatory measure affects a large number of property owners, where it is taken in the interest of social justice or forms part of a large-scale economic reform (Kriebaum, 2007b, p. 740).

This approach merits attention as an award of full compensation may affect the welfare of the State and its public finances to a significant extent, especially in the case of less developed countries. This is particularly so when a country undertakes large-scale nationalizations as part of a broader economic reform in the interests of social justice. While it might prove difficult to formulate specific legal guidance in this respect in an IIA, this issue could form part of broader equitable considerations that may be taken into account when assessing the amount of compensation due.

In the IIA context, the differences between compensation and reparation include:

(a) Restitution of the expropriated property is a remedy available only for unlawful takings, although this appears to be only a theoretical difference;

(b) There may be consequential losses different from loss of profits and not linked to the property's value at the moment of the expropriation;

(c) If the value of the expropriated investment has increased between the date of the taking and the date of the arbitral decision, this increased value is to be awarded.

In *ADC v. Hungary*, the tribunal noted that the investment's value had risen considerably after the expropriation, and therefore considered that "*the application of the Chorzów standard requires that the date of valuation should be the date of the Award and not the date of expropriation, since this is what is necessary to put the Claimants in the same position as if the expropriation had not been committed*".[9] This approach could not be adopted in the context of a lawful taking where treaties require that the investment be valued at the date immediately before the taking. The *ADC v. Hungary* case is exceptional because the value of the property rarely increases after the expropriation.

Under the *Chorzów* rule, a claimant is free to request whatever it believes will serve to re-establish the situation as if the wrongful act never occurred. For instance, in addition to the loss of future profits, investors have claimed, inter alia, moral damages, incidental expenses (e.g. costs of removing the personnel from a foreign country, costs incurred in liquidating the company established to operate the investment) and attorney's fees.

While in theory there is a distinction between compensation for lawful expropriations and reparation for unlawful ones, the typical approach is to award an investment's fair market value, regardless of the type of expropriation. States may wish to reconsider or clarify the applicable treaty rules in order to give tribunals an opportunity to integrate equitable considerations and avoid excessive compensations in case of lawful expropriations.

B.   Valuation of investments

The method that is chosen to value an expropriated investment may have a significant impact on the amount awarded.

Valuation of an investment is required in cases of both lawful and unlawful expropriation. The fair market value of an asset represents the price that a seller would be willing to accept and a buyer would be willing to pay for it in an arm's length transaction. Given the hypothetical nature of the modelled transaction (the investment has been expropriated and not bought on the market), any valuation will display some measure of uncertainty and imprecision. In light of the international-law prohibition on the award of speculative damages, the task of an arbitral tribunal, and of the valuation experts assisting it, is to reduce the degree of uncertainty as much as possible.

The task is relatively straightforward if there exists an active market for the type of asset concerned (e.g. real estate) and, accordingly, many comparable transactions. When the investment is a going concern for which a stream of profits is expected, such as a long-term concession, the exercise becomes more complex.

There are many different techniques in order to estimate the value of an investment and no single valuation method that would suit all circumstances. Valuation methods can be grouped in two main categories: (a) backward-looking techniques that rely on the historic cost of an investment or (b) forward-looking techniques that estimate the market value of an investment based upon its ability to generate profits.

The World Bank Guidelines provide a useful description of the principal valuation methods as well as the circumstances in which a particular method is likely to be relevant (see box 13). The subject of investment valuation in the context of IIA disputes has been also addressed in detail in several recent monographs (see Kantor, 2008; Marboe, 2009; Ripinsky with Williams, 2008).

Just as some see the net book value and liquidation value as appropriate methods, as they are reliable and non-speculative, others argue that such methods should provide only a minimum starting point of valuation. The use of the discounted cash flow method has been a particularly contentious issue. Some have argued that:

Box 13. Methods of valuation according to the World Bank Guidelines on the Treatment of Foreign Direct Investment (1992)		
Method	Description	When?
Discounted cash flow value	Receipts realistically expected from the enterprise in each future year of its economic life as reasonably projected minus that year's expected cash expenditure, after discounting this net cash flow for each year by a factor which reflects the time value of money, expected inflation and the risk associated with such cash flow under realistic circumstances. Such discount rate may be measured by examining the rate of return available in the same market on alternative investments of comparable risk on the basis of their present value.	For a going concern with a proven record of profitability.[10]

/...

Box 13. (concluded)		
Liquidation value	Amounts at which individual assets comprising the enterprise or the entire assets of the enterprise could be sold under conditions of liquidation to a willing buyer less any liabilities which the enterprise has to meet.	For an enterprise which, not being a proven going concern, demonstrates lack of profitability.
Replacement value	Cash amount required to replace the individual assets of the enterprise in their actual state as of the date of the taking.	When value has been recently assessed or has been determined as of the date of the taking and can therefore be deemed to represent a reasonable replacement value.
Book value	Difference between the enterprise's assets and liabilities as recorded on its financial statements or the amount at which the taken tangible assets appear on the balance sheet of the enterprise, representing their cost after deducting accumulated depreciation in accordance with generally accepted accounting principles.	Idem.

"The discounted cash flow method is in essence a speculation about the future dressed up in the appearance of mathematical equations. The difficulty with this method – as compared to the historic cost method – is that while it may look objective and scientific when presented by experts using spreadsheet models, it does not provide objective and predictable outcomes." (Wälde and Sabahi, 2007, p. 19.)

At the same time, the DCF method is commonly used by the markets to value investments, provided there is sufficient and reliable information for projecting future cash flows.

In most cases, the DCF analysis will generate a higher value than the historic-cost or asset-based methods (book value, liquidation value or replacement value). However, this is not always so. In one decided case, the historic costs of the investment at issue were in the region of $20 million, while the DCF analysis showed that the investment was worth zero as it had no prospect of profitable operations – the tribunal followed the DCF methodology and did not award any compensation.[11]

The difficulty of opting for the DCF method stems from the fact that international rules on responsibility of States prohibit compensation for speculative or uncertain damage. Given that the DCF method always implies projections of cash flows into the future, some consider this method speculative and thus inappropriate in the arbitration context. On the other hand, it has been pointed out that *"[s]peculation and uncertainty, inherent in any DCF analysis, can be dealt with by taking conservative estimates of cash flow projections and application of a higher discount rate"*. (Ripinsky with Williams, 2008, p. 211)

In general, tribunals have exercised caution with awarding lost future profits and, accordingly, with the DCF method of valuation. In *SPP v. Egypt*, the tribunal considered that DCF method was inappropriate because the project was in its infancy and there was very little history on which to base projected revenues. The tribunal noted that only 386 lots (about 6 per cent of the total) had been sold when the project had been cancelled.[12] In *Metalclad v. Mexico,* the tribunal rejected the DCF valuation as the business at issue (waste landfill) was never operative, holding that *"where the enterprise has not operated for a sufficiently long time to establish a performance record or where it has failed to make a profit, future profits cannot be used to determine going concern or fair market value"*.[13] In *Tecmed v. Mexico*, the tribunal rejected the DCF method as the landfill had operated as an ongoing business for a short period (two and a half years) and there was no sufficient historical data to prepare reliable estimates.[14] In *Siemens v. Argentina*, the tribunal rejected the claim for lost profits having considered that they were unlikely to ever have materialized.[15] In *Vivendi v. Argentina II*, the tribunal held that the claimant had failed to establish with a sufficient degree of certainty that the expropriated concession would have been profitable.[16] In *Clorinda Vecchi v. Egypt*, the tribunal rejected the DCF valuation as the project was in an early stage of development and lacked a track record of established trading.[17]

However, tribunals have applied the DCF method in other cases.[18] Arbitral practice reveals that the appropriateness of a particular method is largely determined by the circumstances surrounding an investment at issue and information available. Much depends on the characteristics of the investment, its proven track record of profitable operations and the available market references.

Moreover, as all methods have virtues and flaws, and given that they are not mutually exclusive, tribunals are more likely to be persuaded by a number of different valuation techniques that generate comparable figures. If the results shown by different methods are highly divergent, these differences can either be rationally explained or should suggest that there are errors or unsubstantiated assumptions in one or more of the methods used (Ripinsky with Williams 2008, p. 235).

Tribunals often encounter difficulties when it comes to determining the quantum of compensation. Valuation is a highly technical enterprise, which requires specialized knowledge and skills. The disputing parties, with the help of their valuation experts, often overstate or minimize the damages suffered in order to pursue their own interests. On some occasions, tribunals have ended up awarding damages at mid-point or engaging in an ex-post facto rationalization of the amount that seemed reasonable in the circumstances. These reasons result in a rather loose system with a wide margin of discretion left to arbitrators. As discussed above, some IIAs have sought to limit this discretion, in particular by providing that future profits are not recoverable (see section I.F.4(iv)).

Notes

[1] *The Factory at Chorzów* (Claim for Indemnity) (The Merits), *Germany v. Poland*, Permanent Court of International Justice, Judgment, 13 September 1928, 1928 P.C.I.J. (ser. A) No. 17, p. 47.

[2] Ibid.

[3] *"[A]* clear distinction must be made between lawful and unlawful expropriations, since the rules applicable to the compensation to be paid by the expropriating State differ according to the legal characterization of the taking." (*Amoco v. Iran*, Award, 14 July 1987, para. 192.)

[4] *ADC v. Hungary*, Final Award, 2 October 2006, para. 481.

[5] *Siemens v. Argentina*, Award, 6 February 2007, para. 352.

[6] *Vivendi v. Argentina II*, Award, 20 August 2007, paras. 8.2.3–8.2.6.

[7] United Nations General Assembly Resolution 1803 (XVII), 14 December 1962, Declaration on Permanent Sovereignty over Natural Resources, para. 4. For the relevant scholarly interpretations, see, for example, Lauterpacht, 1990, p. 249.

[8] *The Factory at Chorzów (Claim for Indemnity) (The Merits), Germany v. Poland,* Permanent Court of International Justice. Judgment, 13 September 1929, 1928 P.C.I.J. (ser. A) No. 17, p. 47. The Chorzów Factory case is different from most modern disputes because the Government of Poland had undertaken an explicit commitment not to expropriate the factory. The Court found that Poland's act of seizing the factory was a violation of this international commitment; it was "not an expropriation – to render which lawful only the payment of fair compensation would have been wanting, it [wa]s a seizure of property rights and interests which could not be expropriated even against compensation" (Ibid., p. 46).

[9] *ADC v. Hungary,* Award, 2 October 2006, para. 497.

[10] The World Bank Guidelines define a going concern as an enterprise consisting of income-producing assets which has been in operation for a sufficient period of time to generate the data required for the calculation of future income and which could have been expected with reasonable certainty, if the taking had not occurred, to continue

producing legitimate income over the course of its economic life in the
general circumstances following the taking by the State.

[11] *Biwater v. Tanzania,* Award, 24 July 2008.

[12] *SPP v. Egypt,* Award on the Merits, 20 May 1992, para. 36.

[13] *Metalclad v. Mexico,* Award, 30 August 2000, para. 120.

[14] *Tecmed v. Mexico,* Award, 29 May 2003.

[15] *Siemens A.G. v. Argentina,* Award, 6 February 2007.

[16] *Vivendi v. Argentina II,* Award, 20 August 2007.

[17] *Siag and Vecchi v. Egypt,* Award, 1 June 2009.

[18] See, for example, *ADC v. Hungary,* Award, 2 October 2006; *CMS v.
Argentina,* Award, 12 May 2005; *CME v. Czech Republic,* Final
Award, 14 March 2003.

IV. POLICY OPTIONS

The policy choices with respect to expropriation provisions can be grouped into three main models – a "high protection" model, an "increased predictability" model and a "qualified" model. The high protection model is more or less uniform and can be found in many existing treaties. The "increased predictability" model refers to the clarifications of the type introduced by Canada and the United States in their model BITs in 2004, which give additional guidance as regards indirect expropriation and reaffirm the right to regulate. Finally, there is the "qualified" model, which may feature a variety of limitations and qualifications to the expropriation provision in order to respond to States' particular policy objectives and concerns. The three models are discussed in turn.

A. High protection model

Under the "high protection" model, the contracting States seek to maximize the protective effect of the treaty, i.e. to ensure a wide protection against all kinds of expropriations and nationalizations. This approach can be found in most existing investment treaties concluded before the wave of ISDS cases. A typical clause contains a prohibition against direct and indirect expropriation of investments unless for a public purpose, on a non-discriminatory basis, under due process of law and upon payment of compensation, which shall be prompt (without delay), adequate (fair market value) and effective (freely convertible and transferable currency). The expropriation article would be accompanied by a broad, non-exhaustive definition of investment, covering classical forms of property rights, but also other notions such as contracts, licences, concessions, claims to money and intangible rights.

This approach does not contain any qualifiers and limitations of any sort and in some circumstances may lead to unintended consequences as a result of its breadth. It facilitates an expansive understanding of the notion of indirect expropriation, including the coverage of interests that are not necessarily property rights formed under domestic law. It does not offer clarity as to the elements to be taken into account when drawing a line between expropriation and non-compensable regulation.

Countries that are primarily capital exporters may prefer this model to the extent that it provides maximum protection to their foreign investors, although they may be concerned that their own regulatory measures may be contested before international tribunals. From the point of view of developing countries, adherence to this strict model could stem from a desire to attract and retain foreign investment. However, a high protection expropriation provision, on its own, would hardly contribute to such purpose.

Possible formulation

1. Investments of investors of either Contracting Party in the territory of the other Contracting Party shall not be nationalized, expropriated or subjected to measures having equivalent effect to nationalization or expropriation (hereinafter referred to as "expropriation") except for a public purpose, in accordance with due process of law, on a non-discriminatory basis and against the payment of prompt, adequate and effective compensation.

2. Such compensation shall amount to the market value of the expropriated investment immediately before the expropriation or before the impending expropriation became publicly known, whichever is earlier.

3. Such market value shall be expressed in a freely convertible currency. Compensation shall include interest at a commercial rate from the date of expropriation until the date of payment. Compensation shall be paid without delay, be effectively realizable and freely transferable.

B.   Increased-predictability model and reaffirming the right to regulate

The increased-predictability model does not purport to modify the default rules of the customary international law of expropriation. Rather, it seeks to clarify the law in order to give additional guidance to the parties and arbitrators and to ensure its correct and consistent application. It was introduced by Canada and the United States after these countries had to face a series of investors' expropriation claims brought under NAFTA.

The relevant clarifications concern three main issues: (a) definitions of direct and indirect expropriation, (b) factors that help establishing indirect expropriation and (c) criteria that help distinguish between indirect expropriation and non-compensable regulation.

1.   Definitions of direct and indirect expropriation

Negotiators may wish to clarify what is understood by direct and indirect taking. This can be helpful because the text identifies the possible methods of a direct taking (formal transfer of title and outright seizure) and, more importantly, indicates that the effect of an indirect expropriation must be equivalent to the effect of a direct one, i.e. that it must amount to a total or near-total deprivation.

Possible formulation

Expropriation may be either direct or indirect:

(a) Direct expropriation occurs where an investment is nationalized or otherwise directly expropriated through formal transfer of title or outright seizure;

(b) Indirect expropriation occurs where a measure or series of measures by a Party has an effect equivalent to direct expropriation without formal transfer of title or outright seizure.

2.   Establishing indirect expropriation

The treaty may clarify the criteria to be used in making determinations of whether an indirect taking has occurred. These criteria are to be used in combination, as part of a global assessment, and on a case-by-case basis. It is typically emphasized that the adverse effect on the value of an investment on its own is not sufficient to find an expropriation (rejection of the "sole effects" doctrine). In addition, given the uncertainty about the possible sources of investors' legitimate expectations, a State may need to clarify that issue (e.g. by establishing that legitimate expectations may arise only from the State's written commitments to the specific investor). Finally, the "character" of a measure refers to its nature, purpose and specific characteristics, which are particularly important with respect to regulatory acts.

Possible formulation

The determination of whether a measure or series of measures of a Party constitute an indirect expropriation requires a case-by-case, fact-based inquiry that considers, among other factors:

(a) The economic impact of the measure or series of measures, although the sole fact that a measure or series of measures of a Party has an adverse effect on the economic value of an investment does not establish that an indirect expropriation has occurred;

(b) The extent to which the measure or series of measures interfere with distinct, reasonable investment-backed expectations [arising out of the Party's prior binding written commitment to the investor]; and

(c) The character of the measure or series of measures.

3.   Distinguishing between indirect expropriation and non-compensable regulation

It is common ground that the expropriation provision should not be read as curbing police powers of the host State and its right to regulate to achieve public-welfare objectives. To reaffirm a State's right to regulate without paying compensation, a significant number of countries have taken the approach of including specific treaty language.

Generally, the relevant factors are the nature of the measure (whether it is a bona fide regulatory act), its purpose (whether it genuinely pursues a legitimate public policy objective) and specific characteristics (whether the measure is non-discriminatory and adopted in accordance with due process). However, there can be different formulations, some of which are unconditional, others leave room for exceptions and still others introduce additional criteria such as proportionality between the measure's objective and the harm inflicted on an investor.

Possible formulation 1 (unconditional)

Non-discriminatory regulatory actions by a Party that are designed and applied to protect legitimate public welfare objectives, such as public health, safety, and the environment, do not constitute indirect expropriations.

Possible formulation 2 (with room for exceptions)

Except in rare circumstances, non-discriminatory regulatory actions by a Party that are designed and applied to protect legitimate public welfare objectives, such as public health, safety, and the environment, do not constitute indirect expropriations.

Possible formulation 3 (with exceptions defined)

Except in rare circumstances, such as when a measure or series of measures are so severe in the light of their purpose that they cannot be reasonably viewed as having been adopted and applied in good faith, non-discriminatory measures of a Party that are designed and applied to protect legitimate public welfare objectives, such as health, safety and the environment, do not constitute indirect expropriation.**Possible formulation 4 (with additional criteria)**

Non-discriminatory measures that the Contracting Parties take for reasons of public purpose or social interest including for reasons of public health, safety, and environmental protection, which are **taken in good faith, which are not arbitrary and which are not disproportionate in light of their purpose**, shall not constitute indirect expropriation.

C. Qualified model

Recent experience shows that it may be prudent for States to minimize certain risks that arise from an overly broad expropriation provision. Some States have been taking steps in this direction and, by doing so, have been qualifying the expropriation disciplines in various ways. The sections below highlight some of the approaches that may be taken in order to address the relevant concerns.

1.   Interests capable of being expropriated

Broad interpretation of the scope of economic interests capable of being expropriated may deviate from the original intention of the contracting States, clash with domestic tradition and complicate the process of valuation. States could consider making it explicit that only "property rights", a narrower term than "investment", are capable of being expropriated. As an option, "property interests in an investment" could be added.

Possible formulation

An action or a series of actions by a Party cannot constitute an expropriation unless it interferes with a tangible or intangible property right [or property interest in an investment].

As a more general matter, it is important to pay special attention to the definition of "investment" in the treaty and exclude from it those types of assets that the contracting parties conclude should not fall under the protection of the treaty, such as claims arising from purely commercial contracts; trade finance operations; short-term loans; public debt securities; bonds of, and loans to, State enterprises; and portfolio investment (see UNCTAD, 2011, pp. 29–34).

2.   Scope of application of the expropriation provision

States may wish to explicitly exempt from the purview of the expropriation provision measures in certain sensitive areas where regulatory activity is particularly strong. This can be done by means of general exceptions that apply to the treaty as a whole or by specific exceptions to the expropriation article.

2.1.   General exceptions

A growing number of treaties include general exceptions (UNCTAD 2010, pp. 86-87). If a tribunal establishes that the challenged measure falls within one of the general exceptions, it would appear that a State cannot be held liable for violating substantive protections of the treaty, including the expropriation article. The details of application of general exceptions to an expropriation clause are yet to emerge in arbitral decisions.

Possible formulation

1. Subject to the requirement that such measures are not applied in a manner that would constitute arbitrary or unjustifiable discrimination between investments or between investors, or a disguised restriction on international trade or investment, nothing in this Agreement shall be construed to prevent a Contracting Party from adopting or enforcing measures necessary [designed]:
   a. To protect human, animal or plant life or health;
   b. To protect public morals;
   c. To ensure compliance with laws and regulations that are not inconsistent with the provisions of this Agreement; or
   d. For the conservation of living or non-living exhaustible natural resources.
2. Nothing in this Agreement shall be construed to prevent a Contracting Party from adopting or maintaining reasonable measures for prudential reasons, such as:

(a) The protection of investors, depositors, financial market participants, policy holders, policy claimants, or persons to whom a fiduciary duty is owed by a financial institution;

(b) The maintenance of the safety, soundness, integrity or financial responsibility of financial institutions; and

(c) Ensuring the integrity and stability of a Contracting Party's financial system.

3. The provisions of this Agreement shall not apply to investments in ... industries.

Furthermore, it is possible to completely exclude particular subject areas, such as taxation, from the treaty's scope. (Note, however, that some countries, while choosing to generally exclude taxation from the scope of the treaty, prefer to submit taxation to the disciplines of the expropriation provision.)

Possible formulation (full exclusion of tax measures)

Nothing in this agreement applies to taxation measures.

2.2.   Specific exceptions

The practice of incorporating specific exceptions or carve-outs applicable to the expropriation provision is not widespread. However, there are some examples showing otherwise.

One exception found in certain treaties relates to the intellectual property rights (IPRs) regime under the WTO Agreement on Trade-Related Aspects of Intellectual Property Rights, commonly known as the TRIPS Agreement. This exception concerns a narrow situation concerning compulsory licences and aims to ensure that the issuance of such licences is not seen as expropriating the investors' IPRs (the latter are routinely included in the definition of investment in IIAs).

Possible formulation

The provisions of this Article [Expropriation] shall not apply to the issuance of compulsory licences granted in relation to intellectual property rights, or to the revocation, limitation or creation of intellectual property rights, to the extent that such issuance, revocation, limitation or creation is consistent with the WTO Agreement.

Some agreements, including NAFTA and the Canadian and United States model BITs, establish that a preliminary procedure has to be followed before a taxation measure may be challenged as being expropriatory. Before bringing an expropriation claim in ISDS proceedings with respect to such as measure, an investor must notify the taxation authorities of the contracting parties. If the taxation authorities agree that the measure is not an expropriation, the claim may not go further. It can only be raised before the tribunal if the tax authorities fail to agree whether the measure is expropriatory or not within a specified period of time (e.g. 180 days).

Possible formulation

A claimant that asserts that a taxation measure involves an expropriation may submit a claim to arbitration only if:

(a)   The claimant has first referred to the competent tax authorities of both Parties in writing the issue of whether that taxation measure involves an expropriation; and

(b)   Within ... days after the date of such referral, the competent tax authorities of the Contracting Parties fail to agree that the taxation measure is not an expropriation.

3.   Compensation and reparation

Compensation and reparation is another issue that warrants close attention. The current rules on compensation are very rigid and require payment of the full market value of the expropriated investment even in cases of lawful expropriations.

Compensation could accommodate a balancing of relevant interests, if a tribunal had flexibility to award less than the investment's full market value where the measure, while ultimately expropriatory, is at least partially explained by legitimate considerations or there are other mitigating circumstances or equitable considerations.

In this respect, States may consider the following options:

(a) Limiting or prohibiting the award of lost future profits, including when this is done through a forward-looking valuation method such as the discount cash flow analysis.

Possible formulation

Compensation shall be limited to direct losses and may not include loss of future profits or be calculated using a valuation method based on the present value of future cash flows.

(b) Clarifying that an (indirect) expropriation may not be declared unlawful on the sole basis that compensation was not paid for it. Consequently, a tribunal that has established that an expropriation had occurred (but no compensation was paid) should calculate compensation by reference to the rules relating to lawful expropriations.

Possible formulation

The sole fact of not paying compensation in accordance with this Article does not render an (indirect) expropriation inherently unlawful.

(c) Allowing tribunals to award – in case of lawful expropriations – less than full market value of an investment when this is supported by the circumstances of a specific case and equitable considerations. This could allow considering *inter alia* the burden which full compensation would entail for the country's public finances, or, if taken further, a country's level of development.

Possible formulation

The compensation shall be determined in accordance with the generally recognized principles of valuation and equitable principles taking into account, inter alia, the capital invested, depreciation, capital already repatriated, replacement value and other relevant factors.

(d) Establishing the limits of reparation for unlawful expropriations, for example by excluding punitive or moral damages.

Possible formulation

A tribunal may not order a disputing Party to pay punitive damages or compensation for moral damages.

(e) Providing that following upon the decision on liability, the disputing parties shall have a period of time in order to agree upon the appropriate means of compensation or reparation, after which, if no agreement has been reached, the tribunal would proceed to determine the quantum.

Even though the promptness and effectiveness requirements have so far not caused serious concerns, some preventive steps may be taken on this respect as well. For instance:

(a) Establishing justifications for delayed payment, such as severe budgetary or foreign exchange difficulties, subject to payment of reasonable interest and adequate guarantees;

(b) Allowing payment in local currency and establishing exceptions to the freely transferable rule.

CONCLUSIONS

The right to expropriate is an undisputed prerogative of sovereign States. This right is, however, conditioned by principles of international law as well as by domestic law in most States, in the sense that the taking must be for a public purpose, on a non-discriminatory basis, under due process of law and upon payment of compensation. The meaning of each of these requirements, which display a high degree of convergence in treaty practice, has been discussed in this paper.

In the pre-IIA era when direct expropriations prevailed, the international debate focused on the amount of compensation to be paid under general international law. Proliferation of IIAs, each providing a specific standard of compensation, has largely put an end to this discussion. In recent times, the notion of indirect expropriation came to the fore due the regulatory activism of the modern State. Today States often intervene in economic affairs in the interests of general welfare, security, safety, environmental and other public-interest objectives.

International law is clear on two points. First, States have a legitimate right to expropriate foreign property as long as the requirements of legality are met (non-payment of compensation alone should not indicate illegality of the expropriation, at least with respect to indirect takings). Second, States have a legitimate right to regulate in the public interest without paying any kind of compensation. The clash occurs when regulation leads to a total or near-total destruction of an investment.

Expropriation and regulation are different in nature. The former focuses on the taking of an investment; it is a targeted act. The latter is part of the common and normal functioning of the State where impairment to an investment can be a side effect. Expropriation is always compensable, whereas regulation is not. Drawing a line between the two is not easy but is of paramount importance: The international rules on expropriation should not diminish or alter in any degree the ability of States to regulate in the public interest. At the same time, regulation must not be used as a disguised mechanism to expropriate foreign property. Criteria need to be established in order to distinguish between the legitimate right of States to regulate in the public interest and the legitimate right of investors to have their property rights duly protected under international law against expropriation.

A factual inquiry, necessarily done on a case-by-case basis, can be grounded in a common conceptual framework. Various sources, including State practice, jurisprudence and doctrine, show that an assessment of indirect expropriation requires a minimum of three relevant factors, namely (a) the degree of interference or economic impact of the measure, (b) the interference with legitimate investment-backed expectations of the investor and (c) the nature, purpose and character of such measure. Analysing a measure in the light of these three relevant factors will assist in identifying whether the measure is a targeted or irregular act, which would constitute an expropriation, or a normal or common regulation aimed at the general welfare.

Indicators of the irregularity of an alleged legitimate regulatory act include discrimination, violation of due process, lack of genuine public purpose, lack of fair and equitable treatment, manifest disproportionality of the measure, abuse of rights and transfer of benefit to the State. No one particular principle should be conclusive or used in isolation; together they serve as elements of a global assessment that must be made to determine whether a measure is expropriatory or not.

Other critical issues include clarifying the range of interests capable of being expropriated as well as the various approaches regarding compensation and reparation. In general, States have a number of policy options at their disposal in order to address specific concerns, minimize risks and achieve desired policy objectives. When making relevant choices, it is crucial to keep in mind that an expropriation provision should not undermine or weaken the right of States to exercise their police powers and regulatory functions.

REFERENCES

Brower CN and Brueschke JD (1998). *The Iran-United States Claims Tribunal*. Kluwer Law International. The Hague.

Brownlie I (2008). Principles of Public International Law. Seventh edition. Oxford University Press. Oxford.

Cheng B (1953). *General Principles of Law as Applied by International Courts and Tribunals*. Cambridge University Press. Cambridge.

Christie GC (1962). What constitutes a taking of property under international law? *British Yearbook of International Law*. 38: 307–338.

Coe J and Rubins N (2005). Regulatory expropriation and the Tecmed case: context and contributions. In: Weiler T, ed. *International Investment Law and Arbitration: Leading Cases from the ICSID, NAFTA, Bilateral Treaties and Customary International Law*: 597–667. Cameron May Ltd. London.

Cohen Smutny A (2005). State responsibility and attribution: When is a State responsible for the acts of State enterprises? In: Weiler T, ed. *International Investment Law and Arbitration: Leading Cases from the ICSID, NAFTA, Bilateral Treaties and Customary International Law*: 17–45. Cameron May Ltd. London.

Dolzer R and Schreuer C (2008). *Principles of International Investment Law*. Oxford University Press. Oxford.

Dugan C, Rubins N, Wallace D and Sabahi B (2008). *Investor-State Arbitration*. Oxford University Press. Oxford.

Fortier Y and Drymer S (2004). Indirect expropriation in the law of international investment: I know when I see it, or caveat investor. *ICSID Review: Foreign Investment Journal*. 19 (2):293–328.

Geiger R (2002). Regulatory expropriations in international investment law: Lessons from the Multilateral Agreement on Investment. *New York University Environmental Law Journal.* 11(1):94–109.

Kantor M (2008). *Valuation for Arbitration: Compensation Standards, Valuation Methods and Expert Evidence.* Kluwer International Law. Alphen aan den Rijn.

Kingsbury B and Schill S (2010). Public law concepts to balance investors' rights with State regulatory actions in the public interest – the concept of proportionality. In: Schill S, ed. *International Investment Law and Comparative Public Law.* Oxford University Press. Oxford.

Kriebaum U (2007a). Partial expropriation. *The Journal of World Investment and Trade.* 8(1):69–84.

Kriebaum U (2007b). Regulatory takings: balancing the interests of the investor and the State. *The Journal of World Investment and Trade.* 8(5):717–744.

Lauterpacht E (1990). Issues of compensation and nationality in the taking of energy investments. *Journal of Energy and Natural Resources Law.* 8(4):241–250.

Lowe V (2004). Regulation or expropriation. *Transnational Dispute Management.* 1(3).

McLachlan C, Shore L and Weiniger M (2007). *International Investment Arbitration: Substantive Principles.* Oxford University Press. Oxford.

Marboe I (2009). *Calculation of Compensation and Damages in International Investment Law.* Oxford University Press. Oxford.

Newcombe A (2005). The boundaries of regulatory expropriation in international law. *ICSID Review: Foreign Investment Law Journal.* 20(1):1–57.

Newcombe A and Paradell L (2009). *Law and Practice of Investment Treaties: Standards of Treatment.* Kluwer Law International. The Hague.

Nouvel Y (2002). Les mesures équivalant à une expropriation dans la pratique récente des tribunaux arbitraux. *Revue générale du droit international public.* 106(1):79–102.

OECD (2004). *"Indirect Expropriation" and the "Right to Regulate" in International Investment Law.* Working Papers on International Investment. Number 2004/4. Paris.

Paulsson J and Douglas Z (2004). Indirect expropriation in investment treaty arbitration. In: Horn H and Kröll S, eds. *Arbitrating Foreign Investment Disputes.* Kluwer Law International. The Hague.

Perkams M (2010). The concept of indirect expropriation in comparative public law – searching for light in the dark. In: Schill S, ed. *International Investment Law and Comparative Public Law.* Oxford University Press. Oxford.

Reinisch A (2008). Expropriation. In: Muchlinski P, Ortino F and Schreuer C, eds. *The Oxford Handbook of International Investment Law.* 407–458. Oxford University Press. Oxford.

Ripinsky S with Williams K (2008). *Damages in International Investment Law.* British Institute of International and Comparative Law. London.

Ruiz Fabri H (2002). The approach taken by the European Court of Human Rights to the assessment of compensation for regulatory expropriations of the property of foreign investors. *New York University Environmental Law Journal.* 11(1):148.

Schicho L (2011). Attribution and State entities: diverging approaches in investment arbitration. *Journal of World Investment and Trade.* 12(2): 283–298.

Schwartz BP and Bueckert MA (2006). Regulatory takings in Canada. *Washington University Global Studies Law Review.* 5:477–491.

Sornarajah M (2004). *The International Law on Foreign Investment.* Second Edition. Cambridge University Press. Cambridge.

Stern B (2008). In search of the frontiers of indirect expropriation. In: Rovine AW, ed. *Contemporary Issues in International Arbitration and Mediation: The Fordham Papers 2007.* Martinus Nijhoff. Leiden.

UNCTAD (2000). *Taking of Property.* Series on issues on international investment agreements. United Nations publication. Sales No. E.99.II.D.23, E.00.II.D.4. New York and Geneva.

_____ (2004). *International Investment Agreements: Key Issues.* Volume I. United Nations publication. Sales No. E.05.II.D.6. New York and Geneva.

_____ (2007). *Bilateral Investment Treaties 1995–2006: Trends in Investment Rulemaking.* United Nations publication. Sales No. E.06.II.D.16. New York and Geneva.

_____ (2010). *World Investment Report 2010: Investing in a Low-carbon Economy.* United Nations publication. Sales No. E.10.II.D.2. New York and Geneva.

_____(2011). *Scope and Definition: A Sequel.* Series on Issues on International Investment Agreements II. United Nations publication. Sales No. 11.II.D.9. New York and Geneva.

_____ (2012). *Fair and Equitable Treatment: A Sequel.* Series on Issues on International Investment Agreements II. United Nations. Sales No. E.11.II.D.15. New York and Geneva.

Wälde TW and Sabahi B (2007). Compensation, damages and valuation in international investment law. *Transnational Dispute Management.* 4(6).

Weston BH (1976). Constructive takings under international law: a modest foray into the problem of creeping expropriation. *Virginia Journal of International Law.* 16:103–175.

Wortley BA (1959). *Expropriation in Public International Law.* Cambridge University Press. Cambridge.

CASES AND ARBITRAL AWARDS

Unless indicated otherwise, the texts of arbitral awards and decisions can be found at http://italaw.com.

ADC Affiliate Limited and ADC & ADMC Management Limited v. The Republic of Hungary ("ADC v. Hungary"). ICSID Case No. ARB/03/16. Award of 2 October 2006.

AES v. Hungary. ICSID Case No. ARB/07/22. Award of 23 September 2010.

Amco Asia Corporation and Others v. The Republic of Indonesia ("Amco v. Indonesia"). ICSID Case No. ARB/81/1. Award of 20 November 1984.

Amoco International Finance Group v. The Government of the Islamic Republic of Iran, the National Iranian Oil Company et al. ("Amoco v. Iran"). Award No. 310-56-3 of 14 July 1987. 15 Iran-United States Claims Tribunal Reports 189.

Antoine Goetz et consorts v. République du Burundi ("Goetz v. Burundi"). ICSID Case No. ARB/95/03. Award of 10 February 1999.

Azurix Corp. v. The Argentine Republic ("Azurix v. Argentina"). ICSID Case No. ARB/01/12. Award of 14 July 2006.

Bayindir Insaat Turizm Ticaret Ve Sanayi A.S. v. Islamic Republic of Pakistan ("Bayindir v. Pakistan"). ICSID Case No. ARB/03/29. Award of 27 August 2009.

Biloune and Marine Drive Complex Ltd. v. Ghana Investments Centre and the Government of Ghana ("Biloune v. Ghana").

UNCITRAL Arbitration. Award on Jurisdiction and Liability of 27 October 1989.

Biwater Gauff (Tanzania) Ltd. v. United Republic of Tanzania (*"Biwater v. Tanzania"*). ICSID Case No. ARB/05/22. Award of 24 July 2008.

BP Explorations Co. Ltd. v. The Government of the Libyan Arab Republic (*"BP v. Libya"*). Award of 10 October 1973. 53 ILR 297 (1979).

Canadian Pacific Railway Co. v. Vancouver (City). [2006] 1 S.C.R. 227. Available at http://scc.lexum.org/en/2006/2006scc5/2006scc5.html.

Case concerning certain German interests in Polish Upper Silesia (The Merits). Germany v. Poland. Permanent Court of International Justice. Judgment of 25 May 1925. 1926 P.C.I.J. (ser. A) No. 7.

Ceskoslovenska Obchodni Banka A.S. v. Slovak Republic (*"CSOB v. Slovak Republic"*). ICSID Case No. ARB/97/4. Award of 29 December 2004.

Chemtura Corporation v. Government of Canada (*"Chemtura v. Canada"*). UNCITRAL Arbitration (NAFTA). Award of 2 August 2010.

CME Czech Republic B.V. v. The Czech Republic (*"CME v. Czech Republic"*). UNCITRAL Arbitration. Partial Award of 13 September 2001.

CME Czech Republic B.V. v. The Czech Republic (*"CME v. Czech Republic"*). UNCITRAL Arbitration. Final Award of 14 March 2003.

CMS Gas Transmission Company v. The Argentine Republic (*"CMS v. Argentina"*). ICSID Case No. ARB/01/08. Award. 12 May 2005.

Compañía de Aguas del Aconquija S.A. and Vivendi Universal S.A. v. Argentine Republic (*"Vivendi v. Argentina II"*). ICSID Case No. ARB/97/3. Award of 20 August 2007.

Compañía del Desarrollo de Santa Elena. S.A. v. The Republic of Costa Rica (*"Santa Elena v. Costa Rica"*). ICSID Case No. ARB/96/1. Award of 17 February 2000.

Consortium R.F.C.C. v. Kingdom of Morocco. Case No. ARB/00/6. Award of 22 December 2003

Continental Casualty Company v. Argentine Republic (*"Continental Casualty v. Argentina"*). ICSID Case No. ARB/03/09. Award of 5 September 2008.

Duke Energy Electroquil Partners and Electroquil S.A. v. Republic of Ecuador (*"Duke Energy v. Ecuador"*). ICSID Case No. ARB/04/19. Award of 18 August 2008.

EDF (Services) Limited v. Romania (*"EDF v. Romania"*). ICSID Case No. ARB/05/13. Award of 8 October 2009.

Elettronica Sicila S.p.A. (ELSI) v. United States of America. International Court of Justice. Judgment of 20 July 1989.

EnCana Corporation v. Republic of Ecuador (*"EnCana v. Ecuador"*). UNCITRAL Arbitration. Award of 3 February 2006.

Enron Corporation Ponderosa Assets, L.P. v. Argentine Republic (*"Enron v. Argentina"*). ICSID Case No. ARB/01/3. Award of 22 May 2007.

Erkner & Hofauer v. Austria. European Court of Human Rights. Judgment of 23 April 1987. (1987) 117 Eur. Ct. H.R. (ser. A) 39.

Eureko B.V. v. Republic of Poland ("Eureko v. Poland"). Ad hoc arbitration. Partial Award of 19 August 2005.

The Factory at Chorzów. Germany v. Poland (Claim for Indemnity) (The Merits). Permanent Court of International Justice. Judgment of 13 September 1929.

Marvin Feldman v. United Mexican States ("Feldman v. Mexico"). ICSID Case No. ARB(AF)/99/1. Award of 16 December 2002.

Fireman's Fund Insurance Company v. United Mexican States ("Fireman's Fund v. Mexico"). ICSID Case No. ARB(AF)/02/01. Award of 17 July 2006.

Former King of Greece v. Greece. European Court of Human Rights. Article 41 Judgment of 28 November 2002.

GAMI Investments v. United Mexican States ("GAMI Investments v. Mexico"). UNCITRAL Arbitration (NAFTA). Final Award of 15 November 2004.

Gemplus S.A. and Talsud S.A. v. United Mexican States ("Gemplus & Talsud v. Mexico"). ICSID Case Nos. ARB(AF)/04/03 & ARB(AF)/04/4. Award of 16 June 2010.

Generation Ukraine. Inc. v. Ukraine. ICSID Case No. ARB/00/9. Award of 16 September 2003.

Glamis Gold. Ltd. v. United States of America. UNCITRAL Arbitration (NAFTA). Award of 8 June 2009.

Grand River Enterprises et al. v. United States of America. UNCITRAL Arbitration (NAFTA). Award of 12 January 2011.

Gustav F W Hamester GmbH & Co KG v. Republic of Ghana (*"Hamester v. Ghana"*). ICSID Case No. ARB/07/24. Award of 18 June 2010.

ITT Industries, Inc. v. The Islamic Republic of Iran et al. Award of 26 May 1983. 2 Iran-United States Claims Tribunal Reports 348.

James and others v. United Kingdom. European Court of Human Rights. Judgment of 21 February 1986. Series A. No. 98; (1986) 8 EHRR 123.

Jan de Nul N.V. and Dredging International N.V. v. Arab Republic of Egypt (*"Jan de Nul v. Egypt"*). ICSID Case No. ARB/04/13. Award of 6 November 2008.

Government of Kuwait v. American Independent Oil Company (AMINOIL). Award of 24 March 1982. (1982) 21 ILM 976.

LG&E Energy Corp., LG&E Capital Corp. and LG&E International Inc. v. Argentine Republic (*"LG&E v. Argentina"*). ICSID Case No. ARB/02/01. Award of 3 October 2006.

Metalclad Corporation v. The United Mexican States (*"Metalclad v. Mexico"*). ICSID Case No. ARB(AF)/97/1. Award of 30 August 2000.

Methanex Corporation v. United States of America (*"Methanex v. USA"*). UNCITRAL Arbitration (NAFTA). Final Award of 3 August 2005.

Middle East Cement Shipping and Handling Co. S.A. v. Arab Republic of Egypt (*"Middle East Cement v. Egypt"*). ICSID Case No. ARB/99/6. Award of 12 April 2002.

Norwegian Shipowners' Claims. Norway v. United States of America. Permanent Court of Arbitration. Award of 13 October 1922. 1 RIAA 307.

Nykomb Synergetics Technology Holding AB v. The Republic of Latvia (*"Nykomb v. Latvia"*). Stockholm Chamber of Commerce. Case No. 118/2001. Award of 16 December 2003.

Occidental Exploration and Production Company v. The Republic of Ecuador (*"Occidental v. Ecuador"*). UNCITRAL Arbitration. Award of 1 July 2004.

Eudoro Armando Olguín v. Republic of Paraguay (*"Olguín v. Paraguay"*). ICSID Case No. ARB/98/5. Award of 26 July 2001.

Parkerings-Compagniet AS v. Republic of Lithuania. ICSID Case No. ARB/05/08. Award of 11 September 2007.

Phillips Petroleum Company Iran v. The Islamic Republic of Iran, the National Iranian Oil Company (*"Phillips Petroleum v. Iran"*). Award of 29 June 1989. 21 Iran-United States Claims Tribunal Reports 79.

Pincova and Pinc v. The Czech Republic. European Court of Human Rights. Judgment of 5 November 2002.

Pope & Talbot Inc v. Government of Canada. Interim Award of 26 June 2000.

Pressos Compania Naviera S.A. and others v. Belgium. European Court of Human Rights. Application 17849/91. Judgment of 20 November 1995.

PSEG Global Inc. and Konya Ilgin Elektrik Uretim ve Ticaret Limited Sirketi v. Republic of Turkey ("PSEG v. Turkey"). ICSID Case No. ARB/02/05. Award of 19 January 2007.

Rumeli Telekom A.S. and Telsim Mobil Telekomikasyon Hizmetleri A.S. v. Republic of Kazakhstan ("Rumeli v. Kazakhstan"). ICSID Case No. ARB/05/16. Award of 29 July 2008.

Saipem S.p.A. v. The People's Republic of Bangladesh ("Saipem v. Bangladesh"). ICSID Case No. ARB/05/07. Award of 30 June 2009.

Saluka Investments BV (The Netherlands) v. The Czech Republic ("Saluka Investments v. Czech Republic"). UNCITRAL Arbitration. Partial Award of 17 March 2006.

Scordino v Italy (No.1). European Court of Human Rights. Judgment of 29 March 2006.

Sedco, Inc. v. National Iranian Oil Company. Interlocutory Award No. ITL 55-129-3 of 28 October 1985. 9 Iran-United States Claims Tribunal Reports 248.

Sempra Energy International v. Argentine Republic ("Sempra Energy v. Argentina"). ICSID Case No. ARB/02/16. Award of 28 September 2007.

S.D. Myers. Inc. v. Government of Canada. UNCITRAL Arbitration (NAFTA). Partial Award. 13 November 2000.

SGS Société Générale de Surveillance v. Republic of the Philippines ("*SGS v. Philippines*"). ICSID Case No. ARB/02/6. Decision on Jurisdiction of 29 January 2004.

Siemens A.G. v. The Argentine Republic. ICSID Case No. ARB/02/8. Award of 6 February 2007.

Southern Pacific Properties (Middle East) Limited v. Arab Republic of Egypt ("*SPP v. Egypt*"). ICSID Case. No. ARB/84/3. Award of 20 May 1992.

Sporrong and Lönnroth v. Sweden. European Court of Human Rights. Judgment of 23 September 1982. 52 Eur. Ct. H.R. (ser. A).

Starrett Housing Corporation et al. v. The Government of the Islamic Republic of Iran ("*Starrett Housing v. Iran*"). Interlocutory Award No. ITL 32-24-1 of 19 December 1983. 4 Iran-United States Claims Tribunal Reports 122.

Suez, Sociedad General de Aguas de Barcelona S.A., and InterAgua Servicios Integrales del Agua S.A. v. The Argentine Republic ("*Suez et al. v. Argentina*"). ICSID Case No. ARB/03/17. Decision on Liability of 30 July 2010.

Técnicas Medioambientales Tecmed S.A. v. The United Mexican States ("*Tecmed v. Mexico*"). ICSID Case No. ARB(AF)/00/02. Award of 29 May 2003.

Telenor Mobile Telecommuncations A.S. v. Republic of Hungary ("*Telenor v. Hungary*"). ICSID Case No. ARB/04/15. Award of 13 September 2006.

Tippetts, Abbett, McCarthy, Stratton v. Iran et al. Award No. 141-7-2 of 19 June 1984. 6 Iran-United States Claims Tribunal Reports 28.

Total S.A. v. Argentine Republic. ICSID Case No. ARB/04/01. Decision on Liability of 27 December 2010.

Waguih Elie George Siag and Clorinda Vecchi v. The Arab Republic of Egypt (*"Siag and Vecchi v. Egypt"*). ICSID Case No. ARB/05/16. Award of 1 June 2009.

Waste Management Inc. v. United Mexican States. ICSID Case. No. ARB(AF)/00/3. Award of 30 April 2004.

Wena Hotels Limited v. Arab Republic of Egypt (*"Wena Hotels v. Egypt"*). ICSID Case No. ARB/98/4. Award of 8 December 2000.

Yagtzilar and Others v. Greece. European Court of Human Rights. Article 41 Judgment of 15 January 2004.

SELECTED UNCTAD PUBLICATIONS

(For more information, please visit www.unctad.org/en/pub .)

World Investment Reports
(For more information, visit www.unctad.org/wir .)

World Investment Report 2012: Towards a New Generation of Investment Policies. Sales no.:E.12.II.D.3. $80.
Available from http://www.unctad-docs.org/files/UNCTAD-WIR2012-Full-en.pdf.

World Investment Report 2011: Non-Equity Modes of International Production and Development. Sales no.:E.11.II.D.2. $80.
Available from http://www.unctad-docs.org/files/UNCTAD-WIR2011-Full-en.pdf.

World Investment Report 2010. Investing in a Low-Carbon Economy. Sales No. E.10.II.D.1. $80.
Available from http://www.unctad.org/en/docs//wir2010_en.pdf.

World Investment Report 2009. Transnational Corporations, Agricultural Production and Development. Sales No. E.09.II.D.15. $80. Available from http://www.unctad.org/en/docs/wir2009_en.pdf.

World Investment Report 2008. Transnational Corporations and the Infrastructure Challenge. Sales No. E.08.II.D.23. $80. Available from http://www.unctad.org/en/docs//wir2008_en.pdf.

World Investment Report 2007. Transnational Corporations, Extractive Industries and Development. Sales No. E.07.II.D.9. $75. Available from http://www.unctad.org/ en/docs//wir2007_en.pdf.

World Investment Report 2006. FDI from Developing and Transition Economies: Implications for Development. Sales No. E.06.II.D.11. $75. Available from http://www.unctad.org/ en/docs//wir2006_en.pdf.

World Investment Report 2005. Transnational Corporations and the Internationalization of R&D. Sales No. E.05.II.D.10. $75. Available from http://www.unctad.org/ en/docs//wir2005_en.pdf.

World Investment Report 2004. The Shift Towards Services. Sales No. E.04.II.D.36. $75.   Available   from http://www.unctad.org/en/docs//wir2004_en.pdf.

World Investment Report 2003. FDI Policies for Development: National and International Perspectives. Sales No. E.03.II.D.8. $49. Available from http://www.unctad.org/ en/docs//wir2003_en.pdf.

World Investment Report 2002: Transnational Corporations and Export Competitiveness. 352 p. Sales No. E.02.II.D.4. $49. Available from http://www.unctad.org/ en/docs//wir2002_en.pdf.

World Investment Report 2001: Promoting Linkages. 356 p. Sales No. E.01.II.D.12 $49.   Available   from http://www.unctad.org/wir/contents/wir01content.en.htm.

World Investment Report 2000: Cross-border Mergers and Acquisitions and Development. 368 p. Sales No. E.99.II.D.20. $49. Available from http://www.unctad.org/wir/ contents/wir00content.en.htm.

Ten Years of World Investment Reports: The Challenges Ahead. Proceedings of an UNCTAD special event on future challenges in the area of FDI. UNCTAD/ITE/Misc.45. Available from http://www.unctad.org/wir.

International Investment Policies for Development
(For more information, visit http://www.unctad.org/iia .)

Investor-State Disputes: Prevention and Alternatives to Arbitration. 160 p. Sales no. E.10.II.D.11. $22.

The Role of International Investment Agreements in Attracting Foreign Direct Investment to Developing Countries. 161 p. Sales no. E.09.II.D.20. $22.

The Protection of National Security in IIAs. 170 p. Sales no. E.09.II.D.12. $15.

Identifying Core Elements in Investment Agreements in the APEC Regions. 134 p. Sales no. E.08.II.D.27. $15.

International Investment Rule-Making: Stocktaking, Challenges and the Way Forward. 124 p. Sales no. E.08.II.D.1. $15.

Investment Promotion Provisions in International Investment Agreements. 103 p. Sales no. E.08.II.D.5. $15.

Investor-State Dispute Settlement and Impact on Investment Rulemaking. 110 p. Sales No. E.07.II.D.10. $30.

Bilateral Investment Treaties 1995–2006: Trends in Investment Rulemaking. 172 p. Sales No. E.06.II.D.16. $30.

Investment Provisions in Economic Integration Agreements. 174 p. UNCTAD/ITE/IIT/2005/10.

Preserving Flexibility in IIAs: The Use of Reservations. 104 p. Sales no.: E.06.II.D.14. $15.

International Investment Arrangements: Trends and Emerging Issues. 110 p. Sales No. E.06.II.D.03. $15.

Investor-State Disputes Arising from Investment Treaties: A Review. 106 p. Sales No. E.06.II.D.1 $15

South–South Cooperation in Investment Arrangements. 108 p. Sales No. E.05.II.D.26 $15.

International Investment Agreements in Services. 119 p. Sales No. E.05.II.D.15. $15.

The REIO Exception in MFN Treatment Clauses. 92 p. Sales No. E.05.II.D.1. $15.

Issues in International Investment Agreements
(For more information, visit http://www.unctad.org/iia .)

Fair and Equitable Treatment: A Sequel. Sales No. E.11.II.D.15. $25.

Scope and Definition: A Sequel. 149 p. Sales No. E.11.II.D.9. $25.

Most-Favoured-Nation Treatment: A Sequel. 141 p. Sales No. E.10.II.D.19. $25.

International Investment Agreements: Key Issues, Volumes I, II and *III.* Sales No.: E.05.II.D.6. $65.

State Contracts. 84 p. Sales No. E.05.II.D.5. $15.

Competition. 112 p. E.04.II.D.44. $ 15.

Key Terms and Concepts in IIAs: a Glossary. 232 p. Sales No. E.04.II.D.31. $15.

Incentives. 108 p. Sales No. E.04.II.D.6. $15.

Transparency. 118 p. Sales No. E.04.II.D.7. $15.

Dispute Settlement: State-State. 101 p. Sales No. E.03.II.D.6. $15.

Dispute Settlement: Investor-State. 125 p. Sales No. E.03.II.D.5. $15.

Transfer of Technology. 138 p. Sales No. E.01.II.D.33. $18.

Illicit Payments. 108 p. Sales No. E.01.II.D.20. $13.

Home Country Measures. 96 p. Sales No.E.01.II.D.19. $12.

Host Country Operational Measures. 109 p. Sales No E.01.II.D.18. $15.

Social Responsibility. 91 p. Sales No. E.01.II.D.4. $15.

Environment. 105 p. Sales No. E.01.II.D.3. $15.

Transfer of Funds. 68 p. Sales No. E.00.II.D.27. $12.

Flexibility for Development. 185 p. Sales No. E.00.II.D.6. $15.

Employment. 69 p. Sales No. E.00.II.D.15. $12.

Taxation. 111 p. Sales No. E.00.II.D.5. $12.

Taking of Property. 83 p. Sales No. E.00.II.D.4. $12.

National Treatment. 94 p. Sales No. E.99.II.D.16. $12.

Admission and Establishment. 69 p. Sales No. E.99.II.D.10. $12.

Trends in International Investment Agreements: An Overview. 133 p. Sales No. E.99.II.D.23. $12.

Lessons from the MAI. 52 p. Sales No. E.99.II.D.26. $10.

Fair and Equitable Treatment. 85 p. Sales No. E.99.II.D.15. $12.

Transfer Pricing. 71 p. Sales No. E.99.II.D.8. $12.

Scope and Definition. 93 p. Sales No. E.99.II.D.9. $12.

Most-Favoured Nation Treatment. 57 p. Sales No. E.99.II.D.11. $12.

Investment-Related Trade Measures. 57 p. Sales No. E.99.II.D.12. $12.

Foreign Direct Investment and Development. 74 p. Sales No. E.98.II.D.15. $12.

Investment Policy Monitors

Investment Policy Monitor. A periodic report by the UNCTAD secretariat. No. 7, 16 February 2012. Available from http://www.unctad.org/en/docs/webdiaepcb2012d1_en.pdf.

Investment Policy Monitor. A periodic report by the UNCTAD secretariat. No. 6, 12 October 2011. Available from http://www.unctad.org/en/docs/webdiaeia2011d12_en.pdf.

Investment Policy Monitor. A periodic report by the UNCTAD secretariat. No. 5, 5 May 2011. Available from http://www.unctad.org/en/docs/webdiaeia20115_en.pdf.

Investment Policy Monitor. A periodic report by the UNCTAD secretariat. No. 4, 28 January 2011. Available from http://www.unctad.org/en/docs/webdiaeia20112_en.pdf.

Investment Policy Monitor. A periodic report by the UNCTAD secretariat. No. 3, 7 October 2010. Available from http://www.unctad.org/en/docs/webdiaeia20105_en.pdf .

Investment Policy Monitor. A periodic report by the UNCTAD secretariat. No. 2, 20 April 2010. Available from http://www.unctad.org/en/docs/webdiaeia20102_en.pdf .

Investment Policy Monitor. A periodic report by the UNCTAD secretariat. No. 1, 4 December 2009. Available from http://www.unctad.org/en/docs/ webdiaeia200911_en.pdf .

IIA Monitors and Issues Notes

IIA Issues Note No. 1 (2012): Latest Developments in Investor-State Dispute Settlement. Available from http://unctad.org/en/ PublicationsLibrary/webdiaeia2012d10_en.pdf.

IIA Issues Note No. 3 (2011): Interpretation of IIAs: What States Can Do. Available from http://www.unctad.org/en/docs/webdiaeia2011d10_en.pdf.

IIA Issues Note No. 2 (2011): Sovereign Debt Restructuring and International Investment Agreements. Available from http://www.unctad.org/en/docs/webdiaepcb2011d3_en.pdf.

IIA Issues Note No. 1 (2011): Latest Developments in Investor-State Dispute Settlement.
Available from http://www.unctad.org/en/docs/webdiaeia20113_en.pdf.

IIA Issues Note No. 2 (2010): Denunciation of the ICSID Convention and BITs: Impact on Investor-State Claims.
Available from http://www.unctad.org/en/docs/webdiaeia20106_en.pdf.

IIA Issues Note No. 1 (2010): Latest Developments in Investor–State Dispute Settlement.
Available from http://www.unctad.org/en/docs/webdiaeia20103_en.pdf .

IIA Monitor No. 3 (2009): Recent developments in international investment agreements (2008–June 2009).
Available from http://www.unctad.org/en/docs/webdiaeia20098_en.pdf .

IIA Monitor No. 2 (2009): Selected Recent Developments in IIA Arbitration and Human Rights.
Available from http://www.unctad.org/en/docs/webdiaeia20097_en.pdf .

IIA Monitor No. 1 (2009): Latest Developments in Investor–State Dispute Settlement.
Available from http://www.unctad.org/en/docs/webdiaeia20096_en.pdf .

IIA Monitor No. 2 (2008): Recent developments in international investment agreements (2007–June 2008).
http://www.unctad.org/en/docs/webdiaeia20081_en.pdf .

IIA Monitor No. 1 (2008): Latest Developments in Investor– State Dispute Settlement.
Available from http://www.unctad.org/en/docs/iteiia20083_en.pdf .

IIA Monitor No. 3 (2007): Recent developments in international investment agreements (2006–June 2007).
Available from http://www.unctad.org/en/docs/webiteiia20076_en.pdf .

IIA Monitor No. 2 (2007): Development implications of international investment agreements.
Available from http://www.unctad.org/en/docs/webiteiia20072_en.pdf .

IIA Monitor No. 1 (2007): Intellectual Property Provisions in International Investment Arrangements.
Available from http://www.unctad.org/en/docs/webiteiia20071_en.pdf .

IIA Monitor No. 4 (2006): Latest Developments in Investor-State Dispute Settlement.
Available from
http://www.unctad.org/sections/dite_pcbb/docs/webiteiia200611_en.pdf .

IIA Monitor No. 3 (2006): The Entry into Force of Bilateral Investment Treaties (BITs).
Available from http://www.unctad.org/en/docs/webiteiia20069_en.pdf .

IIA Monitor No. 2 (2006): Developments in International Investment Agreements in 2005.
Available from http://www.unctad.org/en/docs/webiteiia20067_en.pdf .

IIA Monitor No. 1 (2006): Systemic Issues in International Investment Agreements (IIAs).
Available from http://www.unctad.org/en/docs/webiteiia20062_en.pdf .

IIA Monitor No. 4 (2005): Latest Developments in Investor-State Dispute Settlement.
Available from http://www.unctad.org/en/docs/webiteiit20052_en.pdf .

IIA Monitor No. 2 (2005): Recent Developments in International Investment Agreements.
Available from http://www.unctad.org/en/docs/webiteiit20051_en.pdf .

IIA Monitor No. 1 (2005): South–South Investment Agreements Proliferating.
Available from http://www.unctad.org/en/docs/webiteiit20061_en.pdf .

United Nations publications may be obtained from bookstores and distributors throughout the world. Please consult your bookstore or write to the addresses listed below.

For Africa, Asia and Europe:

Sales Section
United Nations Office at Geneva
Palais des Nations
CH-1211 Geneva 10
Switzerland
Telephone: (41-22) 917-1234
Fax: (41-22) 917-0123
E-mail: unpubli@unog.ch

For Asia and the Pacific, the Caribbean, Latin America and North America:

Sales Section
Room DC2-0853
United Nations Secretariat
New York, NY 10017
United States
Telephone: (1-212) 963-8302 or (800) 253-9646
Fax: (1-212) 963-3489
E-mail: publications@un.org

All prices are quoted in United States dollars.

For further information on the work of the Division on Investment and Enterprise, UNCTAD, please address inquiries to:

United Nations Conference on Trade and Development
Division on Investment and Enterprise
Palais des Nations, Room E-10054
CH-1211 Geneva 10, Switzerland
Telephone: (41-22) 917-5651
Telefax: (41-22) 917-0498
http://www.unctad.org

QUESTIONNAIRE

Expropriation: A Sequel
Sales No. 12.II.D.7.

In order to improve the quality and relevance of the work of the UNCTAD Division on Investment, Technology and Enterprise Development, it would be useful to receive the views of readers on this publication. It would therefore be greatly appreciated if you could complete the following questionnaire and return it to:

Readership Survey
UNCTAD Division on Investment and Enterprise
United Nations Office at Geneva
Palais des Nations, Room E-9123
CH-1211 Geneva 10, Switzerland
Fax: 41-22-917-0194

1. Name and address of respondent (optional):

    _____

    _____

2. Which of the following best describes your area of work?

Government	☐	Public enterprise	☐
Private enterprise	☐	Academic or research institution	☐
International organization	☐	Media	☐
Not-for-profit organization	☐	Other (specify) _____	

3. In which country do you work? _____